POSITION
POWER
PURCHASE

Unbreakable Laws
of
Business Credit

Copyright © 2010 by Credo Publishing Company, LLC. All rights reserved.

Editor: Corey P Smith www.coreypsmith.com

Cover Design: Felix Walker

Book Design: Essex Graphix www.essexgraphix.com

Credo Publishing Company
3238 Players Club Circle Hwy.
Memphis, TN 38125

Website: www.coreypsmith.com
E-mail: corey@coreypsmith.com

Printed in the United States of America.

Library of Congress Catalog Card Number: On File

Library of Congress Control Number: On File

ISBN: 978-0-9767208-1-2

This publication is designed to provide accurate and authoritative information with regard to the subject matter covered. It is sold with the understanding that the publisher is not engaged in rendering legal or other professional advice. If legal advice or other expert assistance is required, the services of a competent professional should be sought.

DISCLAIMER

The reader of the Unbreakable Laws of Business Credit acknowledges that the information presented herein may change over time. While the publisher and author(s) have taken care to ensure accuracy of the contents of this book, they make no representation or warranties with respect to the accuracy or completeness of the contents of this book and specifically disclaim any implied warranties or merchantability or fitness for a specific purpose. The advice, strategies, or steps contained herein may not be suitable for your situation. You should consult with a professional where appropriate before utilizing the advice, strategies, or steps contained herein. Neither the publisher nor author(s) shall be liable for any loss of profit or any other commercial damages, including but not limited to special, incidental, consequential, or other damages.

UNBREAKABLE LAWS OF BUSINESS CREDIT

From the Author

The definition of life has many meanings such as the course of existence of an individual; the period during which something is functional; the organic phenomenon that distinguishes living organisms from nonliving ones and the period between birth and death.

The definition of living is the experience of being alive; the condition of living or the state of being alive and the course of human events and activities. Now ask yourself the question, although I exist, am I living? Everything in life that is obtainable is a figment of the imagination. Maybe not your imagination, but someone's imagination. The reason I say that is because all the tangible things that exist in this universe started out as an idea or imagination in someone's mind.

I often say that people are controlled by the things they are afraid to lose, but you cannot lose something that is not real. Houses, cars, clothes, jewelry, money, all those things that we as human beings long for are so easily obtainable, but the problem is most people simply don't know how to capture dreams and turn them into reality. Life is a game and the quality of your living will depend on how well you play the game. In order to play any game, you must know the rules and many of us don't know the rules or even how to play the game. I cannot teach you how to play the game in one book, but I can give you some of the rules.

The number one rule to playing this game of commerce or credit is to recognize and identify yourself as a corporation and your social security number as a taxpayer identification number. Why? You may be asking. The reason why is because that is how the government and all the corporations that extend you credit identify you as a business. You can choose to be your own business or someone else's business simply by how you position yourself in this game. After reading this book you will thoroughly understand how to reinvent yourself by way of starting your own business.

Remember that employment equals voluntary slavery.

Introduction

Stop using your personal credit to establish credit for your business. This book will serve as a tool to assist small businesses and entrepreneurs obtain business credit with and without using their personal credit. Many vendors will check your business credit report before making critical decisions about your company. With my knowledge and years of experience in corporate credit this book will help you to establish business credit without using your own personal credit.

This book will show you how corporate credit can help your company obtain major credit cards, office supply accounts, equipment leases, store credit cards, and commercial lines of credit. In this book you will learn solid business principles that are required to obtain corporate credit for every new company you start. Obtaining new business credit will be simple once you master the skills provided in this book even if your personal credit is poor. This book will also teach you how to set up your new company and the different business structures in creating a new company.

After you have read this book you will understand how to protect your personal assets from that of your business and establish a full credit profile and become a part of the world's largest database with over 100 million businesses. This book is easy to read and gives you step by step instructions on how to establish corporate credit with the assistance of professionals who fees are too high for the average entrepreneur to pay.

Chapter 1

WHAT IS BUSINESS CREDIT?

Business credit is the single largest source of business financing by volume even exceeding bank loans. Business credit is different from consumer credit, angel investor financing, or venture capital financing. This is possible because business credit is credit that is extended between businesses, usually for the purpose of obtaining equipment, goods or services that will eventually be resold or used to generate a profit.

How Do You Get Credit?

When a business grants you credit it is a privilege by the creditor to defer the payment of a debt over time. An example of this would-be consumer credit grantors (e.g. credit card companies); business credit grantors evaluate the creditworthiness of the applicant to

3

determine whether or not to extend credit. This evaluation criterion is based heavily on the applicant's business credit score.

Obtaining credit for a business is a process that should be established over time. The older the company the more options the business will have to establish credit and obtain loans, leases, and alternative financing without the use of a personal guarantee. This process is not easy, but yet it is not impossible.

Business Credit Reporting Agencies

There are three major companies that collect business information and publish it. These are Dun & Bradstreet, Experian, and Equifax business. Dun&Bradstreet is by far the largest, but the other two are catching up quickly. Most lending institutions incorporate the information and use the commercial scoring model that they retrieve from D&B's database.

There are a few other business credit reporting companies, but they're not big players and a business owner won't need to worry too much about them. These include PayNet.

Dun & Bradstreet is the most common, and is used by most vendors to extend lines of credit. Landlords use them to approve office leases as well. Experian is used by many credit card companies and non-traditional business lenders. Equifax is called the "Small Business Financial Exchange" and is the most important for cash lenders such as banks. To concentrate on one and not the others is to have lopsided credibility. A business needs to build business credit with all three of these major credit reporting agencies to achieve genuine credibility.

Dun and Bradstreet

Dun and Bradstreet is the biggest major business credit reporting agency. Commonly known as D&B, the agency provides information on businesses and corporations for use in credit decisions. Dun and Bradstreet is a publicly traded company with a headquarters in Short Hills New Jersey, and trades on the New York Stock Exchange.

D&B currently holds the largest supply worldwide of business information, with over 200 million business records on file. In 2012, D&B reported that 129.4 million of these records referred to active companies that were available for risk, supply, sales and marketing decisions. Another 76.7 million were inactive companies, providing historical information for file matching and data cleansing.

Dun & Bradstreet has a massive presence worldwide. They had over 2 million records on file in 2012, they reported 54,409,439 were from Europe while only 33,282,653 were from North America. Another 12,097,055 records were from Latin America, while only 27,451,196 records were from Asia Pacific. The lowest volume of records on file were in Africa, with only 1,184,582 records on file, and the Middle East, with only 1,008,477 records on file.

Altogether, Dun & Bradstreet reported holding 206,148,055 records in January, 2012. They also reported having over 1 billion in payment and bank experiences. And they reported over 159 million public records on file.

D&B roots can be tracked all the way back to 1841, with the formation of the Mercantile Agency in New York. In 1933 the Mercantile Agency joined with R.G. Dun & Company and became known as Dun and Bradstreet. In 1962 D&B created the DUNS number, currently the preferred method worldwide of identifying businesses.

Dun & Bradstreet offers many products and services to consumers and businesses. Some of these include risk management products such as the Business Information Report, Comprehensive Report and the DNBi platform. These provide current and historical business information, primarily used by lenders and financial institutions to assist in making credit decisions.

D&B also offers sales and marketing products, such as the DUNS Market Identifier Database, Optimizer, and D&B Professional Contacts, all of which provide sales and marketing professionals with business data for both prospecting and CRM activity.

Just as Equifax, Experian, and Trans Union are leaders in the consumer credit reporting arenas, Dun and Bradstreet is the leader in business credit data.

Dun & Bradstreet has a proprietary DUNS Right Quality Process providing quality business information that is the information of their global risk solutions worldwide. The DUNS Right process was created on the basis of four fundamental questions: 1. Is the data accurate; 2. Is the date complete; 3. Is the data timely; and 4. Is the data globally consistent.

To answer these questions, Dun & Bradstreet runs data through a process called DUNS Right, in which data is collected, aggregated, edited and verified via thousands of sources daily. Their ability to turn massive data streams into high-quality business information is one of many factors that set them apart from any other competitor.

D&B first collects data from a variety of sources worldwide. This data is then integrated into their database through their very own patented entity matching system. By applying the D-U-N-S Number and using corporate linkage they enable customers to view their total risk or opportunity across related businesses. D&B then uses predictive indicators to rate businesses' past performance and to access future risk.

They are the leading provider of risk managements, business information, sales and marketing, and supply management decisions worldwide.

Experian

Experian was formerly a division of TRW, an automotive electronics giant. TRW was originally founded in 1901 as the Cleveland Cap Screw Company. They started producing screws and bolts and grew to produce many parts for the aviation and automobile industry.

In the early 1960s, TRW started a consumer credit information bureau, collecting and selling consumer data, and eventually became known as TRW Information Systems. TRW Information Systems continued compiling data and were the first to start offering consumers direct credit report access in 1986.

7

In 1991, rampant problems started appearing with TRW reporting credit data. Thousands of people in Vermont had tax liens inaccurately reported against them. Similar cases started appearing in the entire northeast, forcing the deletion of countless tax liens across the states of Vermont, Rhode Island, New Hampshire, and Maine.

Dozens of law suits were filed against TRW claiming sloppy procedures to create credit files, lack of response to consumer complaints, and re-reporting previously deleted incorrect data. All cases were settled out of court.

TRW then created a database known as the Constituent Relations Information Systems (CRIS). This system's sole purpose was to gather personal data on 8,000 politicians who held opinions on TRW.

In 1996, TRW was purchased from Bain Capital and the Thomas H. Lee Partners for over $1 billion by GUS plc, a private group of investors. It was then combined with CCN, the largest credit reporting company in the United Kingdom. GUS retained the Experian name for their combined credit services subsidiary.

In 2004 Experian continued its growth by purchasing Cheet Mail, a business founded in 1998 offering e-mail marketing software and services. In 1998 Experian also acquired QAS, a supplier of contact data management and identity verification solutions. As a result of their growth, Experian became the first company ever to win the UK Business of the Year award twice, winning in both 2003 and 2005.

Experian continued to grow in 2005 with its purchase of PriceGrabber for 485 million dollars. In 2005 Experian also acquired FootFall, and information provider for the real estate and retail property industries. Experian also spent $330 million in 2005 acquiring LowerMyBills.com.

In 2006 Experian made a big move when it announced its purchase of Northern Credit Bureaus, located in Quebec, Canada. The same year Experian demerged from their British Company, GUS plc and was independently listed on the London Stock Exchange.

Since 2005 Experian has continued to aggressively grow their corporation. In 2007, they purchased a 65% stake in Serasa, a leading credit bureau in Brazil, now the largest credit bureau in the world. Experian continued to purchase software companies that year, including Emailing Solution, Hitwise, and Tallyan.

In 2010 Experian became the first CICRA licensed credit bureau to go live in India, where it continues to supply reports to the Reserve Bank of India's (RBI) guidelines.

Currently, Experian continues to grow at a rapid pace. In 2011, they acquired a majority stake in Computec S.A., a credit services provider in Columbia. They also purchased Medical Present Value, Virid Interatividade Digital Ltda, and Garlik Ltd, expanding their data and marketing reach.

Experian has also become the second largest reporting agency in the business credit world. They provide business credit evaluations for over 27,000,000 small businesses and corporations worldwide. These business records are spread over 80 countries that Experian services. Experian's reach is across four main geographic regions, including North America, Latin America, UK and Ireland and EMEA/Asia Pacific.

Experian's headquarters are in Dublin, Ireland. They have operational headquarters in Nottingham (UK, Costa Mesa (California), and Sao Paulo (Brazil). Experian plc is listed on the London Stock Exchange (EXPN) and in a constituent of the FTSE 100 Index. In March, 2001, Experian claimed revenue for the prior year of $4.2 million. Currently, Experian employs over 15,000 people, working in 41 countries.

Experian's main business focus is on credit information services. These services provide insight and tolls that help businesses target new markets, predict and manage risk, and optimize customer relationships. Experian also offers Decision Analytics, which enable organizations with large customer bases to manage and automate large volumes of day-to-day decisions. Experian's clients include international banks, utility companies, public service providers, and more.

Experian focuses on providing quality data and analytics to businesses to help them better access risk. They possess a massive consumer and commercial database that they manage to help businesses obtain the best and most up-to-date information. They then extract significant extra value with this data by applying their own proprietary analytics and software.

Experian diligently works to maintain their worldwide notoriety and growth. Their main global focus is to increase their global reach by expanding their global network and extending their capabilities into new geographic areas. They focus on innovation and on enhancing their analytics to deliver high value to their clients. They also strive to achieve operational excellence by leveraging their global scale to deploy global products into new markets.

Equifax

Equifax is the oldest and largest credit bureau in existence today. They were originally founded in 1898, 70 years before the creation of TransUnion.

Two brothers, Cator and Guy Woolford, created the company. Cator actually got the idea from his grocery business, where he collected customer's names and evidence of credit worthiness. He then sold that list to other merchants to offset his own business costs.

The success of this tactic led Cator and his brother, Guy, to Atlanta, where they set up what became one of the most powerful industries in existence today.

The Retail Credit Company was born, and local grocers quickly started using the Woolford Service, which expanded rapidly. By the early 1900's, the service had expanded from grocers to the insurance industry.

Retail Credit Company continued to grow into one of the largest credit bureaus, and by the mid 1900's, having nearly 300 branches in operation. They collected all kinds of consumer data, even rumors about people's marital lives and childhoods. They were also scrutinized for selling this data to just about anyone who would buy it.

Throughout the 60's, Equifax continued to provide credit reporting services, but the majority of their business came from making reports to insurance companies when people applied for new insurance policies, including life, auto, fire, and medical insurance. Almost all major insurance companies were using RCC to get information on the health, habits, morals, finances and vehicle use of potential insures.

Equifax also provided companies with services including investigating insurance claims and making employment reports when people were seeking new jobs. Back in the 60s, most of Equifax's credit work was actually being done by their subsidiary, Retailers Commercial Agency.

In the late 60s, Equifax started to compile their data onto computers, giving many more companies access to this data, if they chose to purchase it. They also continued to buy up many more of their smaller competitors, becoming larger and also attracting the attention of the Federal government. They began to earn a bad reputation for selling data to anyone who wanted it, whether or not the data was accurate.

Equifax was gathering details about people including their marital troubles, jobs, school history childhood, sex life, political activates, and more. There was no limit to the kind or amount of data they were collecting. Some of the information was factual, while large swathes of the rest were completely false; some information was literally no more than rumors. Equifax was even said to reward their employees for findings the most negative information about consumers.

In response, when the US Congress met in 1971 it enacted the Fair Credit Reporting Act. This new law was the first to govern the information credit bureaus provided and regulated what they were allowed to collect and sell. Equifax was no longer allowed to misrepresent itself when conducting consumer investigations and employees were no longer given bonuses on the basis of the negative information they were collecting using the standard practice in the past.

Retail Credit Division was charged with violating this law a few years later, causing even more government restrictions to be implemented. Scarred with a bad reputation for violations of the new credit laws, the company changed its name to Equifax in 1975 to improve its image.

Throughout the 1980s, Equifax, Experian and TransUnion split up the remaining smaller credit rating agencies between them, adding 104 of those to Equifax's portfolio. Equifax aggressively grew throughout the US and Canada, and then began growing their commercial business division across the UK. At this time, Equifax started competing more aggressively with rivals Dun & Bradstreet and Experian. They then continued to grow, taking alliance with CSC Credit Services and another 65 additional bureaus.

The insurance reporting aspect of Equifax's model was phased out. At one stage, the company also had a division selling specialist credit information to the insurance industry, but they spun off this service, including the Comprehensive Loss Underwriting Exchange (CLUE) database, as Choice Point in 1997. Choice Point formerly offered digital certification services, which it sold to Geo Trust in September, 2001.

Also in 2001 Equifax spun off its payment services division, forming the publicly-listed company Certegy, which acquired Fidelity National Information Services in 2006. Certegy effectively became a subsidiary of Fidelity National Financial as a result of this reverse acquisition merger. In October, 2010 Equifax also acquired Anakam Inc., an identity verification software company.

Equifax has continued to grow, now maintaining over 401 million consumer credit records worldwide. They also expanded their services to direct consumer credit monitoring in 1999. Today Equifax is based in Atlanta, Georgia, and has employees in 14 countries. They are listed as a public company on the New York Stock Exchange (NYSE) under the sign EFX.

Since its inception, Equifax has operated in the business-to-business sector, selling consumer credit and insurance reports and related analytics to a wide array of businesses worldwide. Equifax reports are still commonly used by retailers, insurance firms, healthcare providers, utilities, government agencies, banks, credit unions, personal finance companies, and other financial institutions.

Equifax provides business credit evaluations for small businesses and corporations, allowing them to detect early signs of trouble by monitoring key customers, suppliers & partners. Equifax offers a business scoring credit scoring model known as the Equifax Small

Business Enterprise. Equifax's model is designed for companies that provide goods and services to small businesses.

Equifax sells business credit reports, analytics, demographic data, and software. Its reports still provide large amounts of detailed information on the personal credit and payment history of individuals and businesses to indicate how they have honored financial obligations.

Equifax's source of data today is still some of the most vital information used by credit grantors to decide what sort of product or services they offer to their customers and at what terms. Equifax's system for collecting data is NCTUE, an exchange of non-credit data including consumer payment history on Telco and other utility account.

Since 1999 Equifax has also been aggressively growing in several other credit-related areas. It has excelled with their credit fraud and identity theft prevention products. Equifax has also started earning a major part of its revenue from services which provide consumers and businesses with credit monitoring.

Today Equifax is one of the major credit reporting agencies used in many countries. Some of the countries where Equifax is mainly used include Canada, Chile, India, Mexico, Peru, the United Kingdom, and the United States.

Chapter 2

BUSINESS CREDIT RATING

The best way to establish a good corporate rating is to build a solid foundation. The philosophy to remember when trying to establish corporate credit is that it is a time-based accomplishment. The biggest mistake that most people make when trying to obtain business credit is thinking that a great personal credit score will qualify the company for a loan. The other mistake is thinking that you need to always use your personal credit to obtain corporate credit.

A good business credit score is only part of the puzzle. The credit score is one of many factors the lender might look at to extend a loan. Just because your company has a 75 to 80 payed score does not prove the corporation's financial ability to repay a large loan.

Also remember that a Corporate Credit Builder program does not shortcut all the information a bank will look at to extend a loan. Loans exceeding $50,000 and large ticket items will always require the corporation to produce financials as evidence to establish the company's ability to pay back a loan. If your corporation has the cash flow and profit, then certainly bank loans, equipment loans, and real estate acquisition are achievable without the use of personal credit. However, if the company is three months old and has established a good paydex score, the score alone will not qualify your company for a loan. The financials and other items will be requested in order for the bank to consider the loan.

Purchasing tangible items such as open lines of credit with companies that provide products and services, obtaining leases, thus on credit while your company is still in the early stages of obtaining business credit from lenders you must have realistic expectations. Just because you have a good personal credit score does not qualify your company for a $100,000-dollar line of credit.

Why Business Owners Shouldn't Use Their Personal Credit?

When officers and owners use their own personal credit to obtain credit for their business they risk the chance of lowering their personal credit scores. There are two reasons business owners should try not to use their personal credit to guarantee business credit. First, the individual signer is liable if the business cannot make the payments and the credit obtained for the business can affect the person's personal credit scores as it relates to amount of available credit used, late payments, and judgments.

Obtaining credit for a business is a process that should be established over time. The older the business the more options the business will have to build credit and obtain loans and leases without the use of a personal guarantee. Even though the process seems time consuming it worth the wait.

How and Why You Should Build a Business Credit Profile

Many small business owners start out using personal savings or assets to finance their business. This can rapidly reach a stage of growth where they are forced to seek credit or investment solutions to fund growth. On the other hand, I am going to teach you how to build your business credit profile in order to assist you in obtaining the financing you need to be successful. As a business owner, ask yourself the following questions:

- Are you looking for a business loan or financing?
- Have you been denied a loan?
- Do you need a business line of credit for working capital or growth?
- Do you want to lease or finance equipment for your business?
- Would you like to stop using your personal credit to guarantee business loans?

As a business owner, the most vital part in the growth of your business is funding. Not only is it important to have the right funding source, it is the most important factor in having a strong foundation for your business.

Business owners quickly realize that applying for business funding is a very complicated process than applying for personal credit. Applying for business funding requires careful preparation. One must understand the demands in the building process and what it takes to qualify. When you apply for business funding, creditors will look at your personal credit and the business credit profile to determine the following: the amount, the terms, and if you will need a personal guarantee.

Example: Let's say you have a personal credit FICO score of 650, but no business credit profile. Based on your personal credit, you are approved for a business loan of $100,000 on terms of 13% interest over 10 years (higher risk to the lender because there is no business credit established). If there was a favorable business credit profile, the terms on the same loan might have been 7% interest over 10 years resulting in the savings of $39,843.60.

Whatever your financing needs are, it is possible to obtain funding for your business. Regardless, if your credit is good or bad, the key in knowing where to go.

When Should You Build a Business Credit Profile?

In order to obtain business financing, you must know where you are right now. You must be aware of what the funding sources is going to look at before you apply. If you don't you are completely wasting your time and will most likely be declined.

In other words, "Pre-Qualify before You Apply."

There are over 4,000 institutional sources of business capital in the United States and each one has different criteria's for funding a deal. Each one of these sources will tell you NO for just one thing. Less than 3% of businesses that attempt to receive funding on their own ever do! If you apply at multiple places without pre-qualifying yourself, you may damage your credit and destroy your chances of receiving funding from sources that would have approved your company.

It is a good idea to start building business credit at least 3 months before your business will need funding. Start by doing a Business Credit Assessment on you and your business. This process can greatly increase your chances of gaining a successful loan approval.

Business Credit Assessment

1. What steps have you taken to build your business credit?
2. What are your personal credit scores?
3. What is your available revolving credit?
4. How old is your business?
5. How many trade references do you have?
6. What amount of business credit are you looking for?
7. How will you use the business credit?
8. How would business credit help your business?

In this book, I will provide many sources that can be used to build vendor credit. These sources are like gold when it comes to business credit building. They are the secret to getting approved for the initial trade lines to start building business credit, establishing a positive business credit score and start getting approved for revolving credit card sources.

Starter Vendor Credit Sources

The following accounts are perfect starter accounts for business credit building. They are great accounts because they work for most businesses, including startup businesses.

1. Radio Shack is great for business credit building. It is one of the nation's most experienced and trusted consumer electronics specialty retailers. Radio Shack offers products most business owners need and want such as computers, phones, batteries, cables and connectors.

Radio Shack is one of those creditors who report to D&B and Experian. It will pull a business credit report to see how the business has paid bills in the past. If there is not enough data on the business credit report, Radio Shack will ask for bank and trade references. This will start the reporting process for a business and place the business on the radar of other lenders.

To be approved, most businesses need to have been in business for at least two years. In addition, they must have a DUNS number and credit references. Like most vendors, Radio Shack offers payment terms of Net 30 for their vendor accounts. Currently, you can call 1-800-442-7221 to get an application. Fill it out, and fax it back to 817-415-3909.

2. Quill sells office supplies, cleaning supplies, packing and shipping supplies, school supplies, printing supplies and more. From filing and storage to hand-held computers, Quill has a wide range of discounted top-name brand products.

Quill reports to B&B. Typically, they require that a business place its first order before being considered for a Net 30 account. If the business has established a D&B score, it will probably get approved with the initial order.

For new businesses with little to no credit history, the business will probably be put on a 90-day prepayment schedule. If an order is made every month for 90 days, they will more likely approve a Net 30 account. New businesses can start out with smaller limits that will increase when bills are consistently paid on time.

3. Laughlin Associates will make sure your business is in corporate compliance with all documents, including Articles of Incorporation, Corporate Minutes, Corporate Resolutions and List of Officers.

Laughlin Associates will approve any business listed in 411, and has a business bank account and an EIN. They report all payments to Experian. It takes 30 to 60 days for the first trade line to show up on the credit report from the date of purchase. They offer low monthly payments, and they report as a Net 30 account.

4. Monopolize Your Marketplace offers a marketing system that teaches businesses how to market their business. They provide

10 audio CDs and over 11 hours of materials that focus on marketing topics, including the marketing equation, MYM technology, industry category strategies, the master marketing letter and more.

Monopolize Your Marketplace is a great starting vendor, as they will approve most businesses for at least $400 vendor credit. They report accounts to Experian and offer Net 30 terms. They offer a payment plan for their system and report the payments receive to Experian. To be approved, a business needs to have an EIN, a real deliverable address and a business bank account.

5. ITC Web Services offers many web and technical services, including website creation. They offer affordable websites and will even revamp a business's current website. They provide Joomla, Drupal, PHP and MySQL website development.

They also help businesses create professional email addresses, web applications, flash animation design, logo design and web banner design, and develop mobile device apps.

6. Business Marketing Services does custom website creation, social media marketing, search engine optimization, logo creation and more. It offers a Net 30 starter vendor credit account and reports to Experian and D&B. Business owners must provide valid proof that their business is operating in the U.S. for them to be approved. Business Marketing Services usually requires 30% payment upfront on purchases and extends credit for the other 70% of the purchase paid over a 5-month period to almost all businesses.

7. Market Click Internet Marketing offers online services, such as search engine optimization and setting up websites, for maximum online exposure. They report to D&B and offer Net 30 terms.

Market Click Internet Marketing gives business credit without requiring any personal guarantee from the business owner and rarely requires a personal credit check. It takes them about 30 to 60 days to report the trade line to D&B.

8. A Printer 4 U offers graphic and logo design services, printing, banner creation and much more. They give most businesses, even startup businesses, a Net 30 credit line of up to $2,500. They report to Experian and D&B. Often, they require a 50% payment upfront on all orders; the business can then finance the rest.

A Printer 4 U requires the business's phone number to be listed in the 411 directories. They also ask for the address, phone number, bank account information and trade references of the business. They require no personal guarantee, and they will approve businesses with no personal credit check from the business owner.

9. Paramount Payment Systems gives businesses the ability to offer payment terms to customers on their products and services. They will accept customers checks from a business, front the business the money from that check, then charge a fee to the customer to collect on those checks; there is no recourse for the business owner if their customer's checks do not clear. With this system, Paramount gives business owners access to funds right away.

Paramount offers Net 30 terms and reports directly to D&B. They do not do business with some industries, such as web design, jewelry, used cars, online businesses, and some basic retail stores.

To be approved, a business must provide an EIN and two years of credit references. They must also show proof on how long they have been in business.

Other Vendor Credit Sources

Many other available vendor accounts come from very well-known companies. However, most require a minimum number of years in operation or established trade lines to qualify such as the following:

1. Staples, mega-retailer that sells office supplies and offers business services, offers a Net 30 reporting business credit trade line that reports to all three business credit reporting agencies.

Staples will check with Experian, Equifax and D&B to see if the business has a credit history. The amount of money they approve a business for depends on the business's established credit history. If the business has no or little credit history, the business owner will typically be asked for a personal credit check and personal guarantee. Staples will also check to see, if the business is listed in the 411 directories and has an EIN.

2. Uline Shipping Supplies is one of the leading distributors of shipping, industrial, packing and janitorial products. They offer a vendor account that can be used for business credit building. This account is offered on Net 30 term and is reported to D&B.

Uline requires every business to have a DUNS number before they can be approved. They will look at the business credit report, searching for existing trade lines, and they might require trade and bank references. They normally want to see at least two trade references and one bank reference.

If they pull a business credit report and see little to no credit history, they will require a few orders from the business to be prepaid before they will offer their Net 30 account. They might also ask for the business's financials.

3. Home Depot is one of the world's largest retailers for home and building supplies. They offer a vendor business credit account on Net 30 terms, and reports to Experian and D&B.

To be approved, the business must have an EIN. It must also have been in business for at least three years. If it has been open for three years or longer, Home Depot most likely will not ask for a personal guarantee from the business owner or require a personal credit check. However, they will require a personal credit check and guarantee front the business owner if the business has been open less than three years.

4. Grainger Industrial Supply is a poplar credit source that thousands of suppliers use for electrical fasteners, fleet maintenance, HVACR hardware, material handling, pneumatics, power tools, pumps and more. They offer a Net 30 account that is reported to D&B quarterly.

If the business has a business license, they will be approved for $1,000 account or less. If the business has trade and bank references, it will be approved for accounts over $1,000. They will require the business to provide an EIN.

27

5. Labor Ready is a leading multinational source of dependable labor for companies across many industries. They offer a vendor account on Net 7 terms and reports to D&B. They require a valid tax ID number and will approve a business for Net 7-day account with no personal credit check or personal guarantee required from the business owner.

6. Sherwin Williams offers a Net 20 vendor account that reports to D&B. They offer a wide variety of products ranging from coatings for plastics, metal and wood to many industries. They will pull both personal and business credit for approval and will typically approve a business with an established, strong credit profile with Dun & Bradstreet.

7. Macy's is a large department store that can supply business with many of the things they may need for employee recognition programs, dress code programs, and special holiday and thank you gifts. Their vendor account is offered on Net 30 terms and is reported to D&B.

Macy's will only approve a business for their vendor account if the business has a positive D&B credit score established. They will compare the business score against the industry average score to determine approval.

They require no personal credit check or personal guarantee from the business owner, but they normally request bank.

8. Budget Car Rentals accounts are reported to Equifax and Dun & Bradstreet, and are approved as Net 30 terms. A business must already have a Budget Express Account for at least two years and spent over $5,000.

For approval, the business must also be listed in the 411 directories and have at least 20 employees.

Building Revolving Credit Made Easy

For the best business credit-building success, a business should obtain at least five revolving business credit card accounts and five vendor accounts. These accounts report to the business credit agencies in different ways and carry more weight than the vendor credit that was initially used to start building the business credit.

After five trade lines have been established and reported, the business will be able to start getting approved for revolving business credit accounts. A revolving credit account is one that allows the business to pay a minimum due per month and not the full outstanding balance. These accounts normally report to Experian, D&B, and sometimes Equifax. Because of how they report, these accounts will help build business credit on a larger scale than the Net 30-day vendor accounts alone do.

Once a business owner has obtained a total of 10 reported accounts, including vendor and revolving accounts, it can then start qualifying for real credit cards through Visa and MasterCard. Of the 10 open accounts, at least one account should have a credit limit of $10,000 or more to qualify for Visa and MasterCard credit.

Most major merchants offer business credit. Many of these accounts offer credit limits of $10,000 or more. A business can get multiple Visa, MasterCard and AMEX cards, and it can continue increasing its limits.

Within a few months of starting the business credit building process, the business will qualify for thousands of real approved credits. Within 6-12 months, the business will have access to over $50,000 in revolving credit with major retailers. Depending on how it utilizes its newly acquired credit, the business can continue to qualify for $100,000 to $250,000 in a year or two.

A business can also secure $50,000 to $150,000 credit lines based on business credit with limited income document requirements. With full income verification, around $250,000 credit lines are available. Most of these credit lines come with check-writing capability and a linked debit card.

Revolving Credit Sources

Many merchants offer revolving credit accounts for businesses. Some of these accounts are starter accounts. These starter accounts are very useful to businesses that are still in the early stage of building their business credit, including those with only a few vendor accounts reporting as trade lines on their business credit. Other accounts might have more stringent requirements for approval than basic starter accounts have.

1. Staples

While the business owner's application is on hold, Staples will verify if the business has an EIN and if it is listed in the 411 directories. They will also check to see if the business name and address match the 411 listing. They will check that the business credit files are open with D&B and Experian.

For businesses with established business credit, they will not require a personal guarantee from the business owner. If no business credit is present with Experian or D&B, Staples will do a credit check on the business owner and will require a personal guarantee.

2. Dell

Business owners visit Dell to buy computers and accessories for their home or business. The Dell Business Credit Account is a popular revolving line of credit that provides an easy way to finance purchases of Dell equipment and reports to D&B.

Dell regularly approves accounts with limits up to $10,000, usually to business owners with a PAYDEX score of 75 or higher. However, a business must have been open for at least six months before they will approve that business. They will sometimes check personal credit during their approval process.

3. Lowe's

Lowe's offers a huge selection of tools, kitchen appliances, cabinets, cabinet hardware, countertops, paint and much more. Customers can purchase online or at their local Lowe's center. It is a popular source of revolving business credit accounts and reports to D&B and Experian.

Lowe's offers a fast-online approval. Applicants with a DUNS number can apply online for approval. They are typically approved for credit limits between $1,000 and $5,000. Unless a good D&B and/or Experian score is established, businesses that have been open less than three years will require a personal guarantor. If the PAYDEX credit score is over 85, they will normally approve the business for credit of $5,000 or more.

Lowes will approve a business for business credit with no personal credit check or guarantee from the business owner so long as the business has been open for three years. If the business has a strong business credit profile and score, they might also approve the business with no personal guarantee required.

4. Office Depot

Office Depot is another mega-retailer that provides office products, office supplies, office furniture, etc. Their revolving account reports to both Experian and D&B.

Office Depot will check the business's credit profile with Experian or D&B before approval. If one business credit reporting agency has no or little information reported, they will check the other credit agency's report. If the business has little to no credit report with either, a personal guarantee from the business owner will be required. Even if a personal guarantee was provided, this account will be reflected in the business credit reports, not in the personal credit reports. The amount approved will depend on the business credit scores they pull. They might also request trade references if there is no business credit score, or if there is limited credit reporting.

5. Wal-Mart

Wal-Mart is one of the best-known retailers in the world. They offer a massive assortment of products, including electronics, toys, home, garden and baby products.

Wal-Mart's account is revolving and reports to both Experian and Equifax. A business should be approved for this account if it has some business credit already established with Equifax and D&B. Wal-Mart requires a business credit score of 75or higher, reflecting that the business pays its obligations as agreed each month. If the business cannot be approved due to limited credit, it can get approved with a personal guarantee from the business owner.

6. Costco Wholesale

Costco Wholesale is an international chain of membership warehouses. They offer an American Express business account with revolving terms that reports to D&B.

Costco looks at the business credit of the business and the personal credit of the business owner with all three credit reporting agencies. Moreover, the business must have an EIN, and the business owner must provide a personal guarantee if the business has been open for less than two years.

7. Amazon.com

Amazon.com is an online shopping company that sells books, magazines, music, videos, electronics, computers, software, apparel and accessories.

They offer their revolving account with no personal guarantee to businesses with an EIN, provided that the business has been open at least three years. They report to Experian, Equifax and D&B.

Depending on the amount of business credit the business already has established, Amazon issues credit limits ranging from $500 to $2,500.

8. Sears

Sears sells a wide variety of products, including appliances, lawn tractors and tools. Their business credit account reports to all three business credit reporting agencies.

They require a good business credit score for approval, and they look at business credit scores from D&B. If there is no score with D&B, they will check with Experian and Equifax.

They do not require a personal guarantee from business owners with established strong business credit scores. In addition, a business must have been open for at least two years and must have an EIN.

Business Credit Gas Cards

Major fuel companies around the country are great sources for business credit gas cards. Business owners can use their gas cards for fuel purchases. These accounts are especially good for truck drivers and other businesses that have vehicles on the road as part of their business model.

1. BP offers a business credit card that reports to D&B and is a revolving credit account. This card can be used in more than 12,500 BP stations around the globe. It can be used for a business fleet's fuel and maintenance needs anywhere MasterCard is accepted.

To apply, a business needs to provide its tax ID number. BP will look at Experian, D&B and Equifax scores. If the business has strong credit profiles and scores, it can be approved with no personal guarantee from the business owner – as long as the business has been open for at least three years.

2. Chevron also offers a great business gas card that is revolving and reports to D&B. Chevron business gas cards can be used at both Chevron and Texaco stations to purchase gasoline, tires, batteries and more.

A business needs a PAYDEX credit score of at least 75 and must have been in business for at least 18 months to be approved with no personal credit check or personal guarantee from the business owner.

3. Speedway Super America's business credit gas card is revolving, and it reports to Experian and D&B. To be approved, the business must have been in business for at least a year.

4. Sinclair Oil also offers a gas merchant account. It is a revolving account that reports to D&B. The account can only be used at Sinclair stations. No personal guarantee or credit check is required from businesses with established business credit history and positive scores.

5. CSI offers a corporate fleet MasterCard account that is accepted at nearly every retail and diesel CSI fueling location. It has over 180,000 stations nationwide. This account is revolving, and it is reported to Experian and Equifax.

CSI requires that 10 accounts be reported on the business's credit reports before they will approve a business for a revolving business credit account. It also requires that one of the trade lines have a credit limit of at least $10,000 before it will approve that business for credit.

CSI requires the business to have an EIN and present all required business licenses, a copy of a voided check, a copy of a utility bill that shows the business address and phone number.

Other Merchant Credit Sources

Before they will approve a business for a revolving business credit account, the following merchants require the business to have an EIN and to present essential documents: all required business licenses, a copy of a voided check and a copy of a utility bill that shows the business address and phone number. Additionally, they require that 10 accounts be reported on the business credit reports.

1. Sam's Club is a warehouse retail chain that offers office supplies, business furniture, vending items, cleaning supplies, paper products, food service supplies, computers and more. It offers a revolving business credit account that reports to Experian and D&B.

2. Key Bank offers a MasterCard credit account. With this account, a business can earn points that can be redeemed for airline travel, merchandise, gift certificates and more. They offer a 0% introductory rate for the first 6 months. This revolving account reports to Experian, Equifax and Transunion.

Key Bank requires that one of the business's trade lines has a credit limit of $10,000 or higher before they will approve that business for credit. They will request a personal credit check and guarantee from the business owner if the business does not match these conditions.

3. Volvo

offers a MasterCard through Wright Express (aftermarket support). It is a great revolving business credit account. This account reports to Experian and Equifax.

Before a business will be approved for credit, Volvo requires that one of the business's trade lines have a credit limit of $10,000 or higher. The business must submit its financials for it to be approved with no credit check or personal guarantee from the business owner.

4. Fleet One Local Fuel Card is a great business credit solution if a business uses cars, vans or trucks. This account if offered on Net 14 terms and reports to all three business credit reporting agencies. This card can be used to pay for vehicle fuel and maintenance.

The Fleet One Local Fuel Card requires that one of the businesses trade lines credit limit is $10,000 or higher before they will approve that business for credit. They will request a personal credit check and guarantee from the business owner if the business does not have the required number of trade lines and credit limit.

Chapter 3

THE BUSINESS CREDIT BUILDING PROCESS

Choose a Company Structure

Regardless of how you choose to operate your business, in order to build a business credit profile, you must have a formal structure. There are six different types of business structures in forming a company:

- Sole Proprietor
- C-Corporation
- L.L.C. Limited Liability Company
- L.L.P. Limited Liability Partnership
- L.L.L.P. Limited-Liability Limited Partnership
- S-Corporation

It is very important to know what type of company you are forming in regards to how much personal liability one has in operating a business.

Sole Proprietorship

Easy to start; owner and business are one in the same; owner is exposed to liability for business debts; if owner conducts business under trade name, a DBA or "Doing Business as" must be filed with the cities or county.

C-Corporation

Owners are called stock or shareholders and ownership is easily transferable; owners are taxed at the corporate and shareholder levels (double taxation); corporation is a separate entity from owners; shareholders are not personally liable for business debts and require filings of Articles of Incorporation with the Secretary of State. S-Corporation; no double taxation; income or loss is passed through to the owners; requires filing Articles of Incorporation with the Secretary of State and IRS form SS-4 (S-Election).

Limited Liability Corporation (L.L.C.)

Limited personal liability of owners; unlimited number of owners; owners pay taxes based on their share of ownership; requires filing of Articles of Organization with the Secretary of State.

Limited Liability Partnership (L.L.P.)

Similar to the L.L.C., but designed for professional organizations such as CPAs and attorneys; requires filing of Articles of Organization with the Secretary of State Limited Partnership. Consists of at least one general partner and other limited partners or general partner is personally liable for the partnership's debts; limited partners are not personally liable, as long as they do not materially participate in the partnership's management; partners are taxed based on ownership percentages and requires filing a Partnership Registration with the Secretary of State. Once you have chosen how you will operate, you need to file your Articles of Incorporation, Articles of Organization, Partnership Agreement or "Doing Business As" with your Secretary of State or your respective Secretary of State. The cost to file will vary.

Limited-Liability Limited Partnership (L.L.L.P.)

The limited liability limited partnership is a relatively new modification of the limited partnership, a form of business entity recognized under U.S. commercial law. An L.L.L.P. is a limited partnership and as such consists of one or more general partners and one or more limited partners. The general partners manage the L.L.L.P., while typically the limited partners only have a financial interest. The difference between an L.L.L.P. and a traditional LP is with respect to the general partner's liability for the debts and obligations of the limited partnership. In a traditional limited partnership, the general partners are jointly and severally liable for the debts and obligations of the limited partnership; limited partners are not liable for those debts and obligations beyond the amount of their respective capital contributions.

Because the L.L.L.P. is so new, its use is not widespread. Arkansas, Colorado, Delaware, Florida, Georgia, Maryland, Nevada, Texas and Kentucky all have adopted statutes that allow for the formation of LLLPs, usually as a conversion of an existing

LP (the general partners might want to do this to reduce their legal liability).

S-Corporation

An S-Corporation is a corporation for all purposes except for taxes. For tax purposes, it is treated very similar to a partnership. This means that S-Corporations don't pay income taxes, but report the results of their operations to the shareholders who report their share of corporate income or loss on their taxes.

Shelf Corporation

Most companies would like to do business with established companies. A company that just opened last week is more likely to default and close down then a company that is an established company and been around for two or more years. Therefore, if you can afford to buy a shelf corporation, it is best to buy a clean unused corporation that has an incorporation date of at least two years old.

A shelf corporation is a corporation that was already formed and waiting to be purchased by an individual or business. Since most new businesses fail, a shelf corp. has the ability to make your business already have beaten the odds of the majority of businesses that fail. This makes banks much more likely to give you higher limits then if your business was just established or less than two years old. If you can afford to buy an existing corporation, make sure you do due diligence to make sure you are not acquiring any liabilities that could come back to hurt you later.

The Advantages and Disadvantages of Business Entities

Advantages of an LLC Relative to a "C" Corporation

Tax Consequences to Owners: The primary advantage of the LLC over the "C" Corporation is in the tax consequences to owners. As a pass-through entity, the LLC's income and losses flow through and are taxed to or deducted by the members, normally retaining the character they had in the LLC. Thus, there is a single level of tax, and losses are fully deductible by members (but are subject to passive activity rules and the deduction may not be in excess of their bases in their membership interests). The income of a C corporation is taxable, both by the federal government and your state, at the corporate tax rate. The corporation and its shareholders may be subject to double taxation, when dividends are paid to shareholders because the corporation pays tax on its income and the shareholders pay tax on dividends received from the corporation and the corporation is not allowed to deduct dividends as an expense.

Structure of the Owners Participation: The owners of the LLC have greater latitude and flexibility in providing for the return of an owner's investment. There is also more liberty in structuring the owner's participation in the enterprise.

Disadvantages of an LLC Relative to "C" Corporation

Retention of Earnings: A venture that intends to retain substantial earnings may find the corporate structure beneficial. It is likely that the marginal corporate tax rate on the retained earnings (only 15% up to 50K) will be lower than the marginal rates applicable to individuals. One needs to carefully study the venture's projections and calculate the estimated after-tax financial performance of the venture before making a decision.

Fringe Benefits: An LLC taxed as a partnership cannot provide many of the fringe benefits that a "C' Corporation can provide. Members are not employees for purposes of the fringe benefit rules. See, e.g., IRC 5105(9) relating to accident and health care plans and IRC #79 relating to group term life insurance. If the LLC provides members with fringe benefits, the cost must be included in the member's gross income. In some states, "C" s can maintain more favorable asset-protected retirement plans.

Advantages of LLC Relative to "S" Corporation

Restrictions on Ownership: An S Corporation offers the advantage of limited liability for owners, and some of the advantages of being taxed as a partnership. It does not pay tax on its earnings, and its profits and losses are passed through and taxed directly to its shareholders. However, there are a number of restrictions on the ownership of and the operation of an S corporation that do not apply to an LLC. The S corporation can have only one class of stock. Its stockholders can be only natural persons and those persons must be U.S citizens or resident aliens. An "S" corporation may have no more than 75 shareholders.

Special Allocations: Further, an "S" Corporation may not specially allocate tax attributes to its shareholders. Those attributes pass through pro rata. This fact restricts the type of debt the corporation may issue, hampers efforts to gradually shift control of family-owned businesses, and in general makes passive investments difficult to structure.

Deductibility of Losses: An "S" corporation differs in the ability to obtain tax basis from its share of the entity's liability, which determines the extent of losses that may be deducted by the owners, and their ability to receive operating distributions tax free. An "S" corporation shareholder does not share in the entity liabilities and its basis is limited to the cash invested. Both an LLC member and a limited partner increase their basis by the allocable share of entity liabilities. Moreover, distributions of appreciated property trigger a gain to the "S" corporation that passes through to the shareholders. Also, there is a second entity level tax on built-in gain, if the "S" corporation was formerly a "C."

Restrictions on Ownership: An "S" Corporation offers the advantage of limited liability for owners and some of the advantages of being taxed as a partnership. It does not pay tax on its earnings, and its profits and losses are passed through and taxed directly to its shareholders. However, there are a number of restrictions on the ownership of and the operation of an "S" corporation that do not apply to an LLC. The "S" corporation can have only one class of stock. Its stockholders can be only natural persons, and those persons must be U.S. citizens or resident aliens. An "S" corporation may have no more than 75 shareholders.

Disadvantages of LLC Relative to "S" Corporation

The LLC offers the limited liability of the "S" corporation and pass-through taxation with none of the "S" corporation restrictions on ownership and operations. Therefore, we really cannot see a great deal of general disadvantage. However, there may be some disadvantages in a special case.

In addition to any disadvantages of LLCs compared to other entities, one should keep in mind the following general drawbacks to the use of LLCs: The legal ramifications of forming and operating an LLC, e.g., tax classification is more uncertain because of the lack of guidance from established case law and regulations. This may be more theoretical than real. Other states may not recognize all of the rights and privileges afforded to an LLC in your home state. If the LLC has one or more members who are non-residents of the LLC state, it must file a list of members and consents with its annual state tax return. As to any non-resident member who fails to consent to your state tax jurisdiction, the LLC must pay the tax attributable to the non-consenting member's distributive share of LLC income. The members of an LLC may have implied authority to act on behalf of the LLC and bind the LLC. E.g. signing of deed of trust (mortgage).

As a general rule, the LLC will probably serve well in those circumstances where the limited partnership and "S" corporation were formerly used. The LLC may even be used in those circumstances where the "C" corporation was used. However, the "C" corporation does have its advantages, particularly with respect to the availability of nontaxable fringe benefits and asset protected retirement plans. Therefore, we recommend you continue to use the "C" corporation in those circumstances where a "C" corporation was formerly used. Use an LLC in those situations were a limited partnership

(FLP, unless a specific estate and gift tax result is desired) or "S" corporation was formerly used.

A shelf corporation, also called an aged corporation, is a corporation that has had no activity. It was created and put on the "shelf" to age. This is the conventional meaning of a shelf corporation but recently we have all been seen shelf corporations being sold with credit files already established. The major reason for acquiring a shelf corporation for building business credit is, some lenders only lend to corporations that are two years old. You really cannot blame the min this current economic climate. If you were a lender, I assure you that you will feel more comfortable lending money to a corporation that has been in business for 20 years than one that has been in business for 6 months. Let's briefly look at what to expect when looking for a shelf corps the conventional way. So, in looking for shelf corporations we have a number of questions.

• What should I look for in a Shelf Corporation?
• Where can I get a Shelf Corporation?
• What should I pay for a Shelf Corporation? When you are done with this book, I am pretty sure that almost everything that you thought you knew about shelf corps will be dispelled.

Buying a shelf corporation can be a pretty expensive purchase so we will like to take every precaution that this corporation is worth it. When purchasing a shelf corporation, you must first get as much information on the corporation as possible. Current Name, Address, Tax ID (if applicable), DUNS Number (if applicable) and telephone number. This will give you the necessary information to check the background of the company. You first want to go to the Secretary of State website of the state the Corporation is formed in and check to ensure that the company is active and up to date with all state fees. Secondly you will need to check the company's credit files at Dun and Bradstreet and Experian Business. You may have to pay for the credit file but if the sources for your shelf corps are not reliable, this will be worth it. It is also better for the corporation to already have a Tax ID number and preferably a DUNS number although getting a DUNS number with a shelf corps is rare.

How to Buy and Build a Shelf Corporation.

We recommend two resellers of shelf corps: Amerilawyer.com. and Wyoming Corporate Services. Shelf corporations are simply aged corporations. Every day, in every state, there are corporations that are being closed. In some situations, an entrepreneur may have started a business and it failed and he simply stopped paying his state fees to keep the corporation active and there are other times when the business did not even get off the ground. This is where you can capitalize. You can go to your Secretary of State website and reinstate these corporations. Much of the company's information and owner's information is available. You can sometimes do a request for documents depending on the state. In most states, you simply have to send in some paperwork and pay for all the yearly fees that the company was inactive. Please see your respective SOS website for more information.

The general rule is $1000 for every year in the company's age. A two-year-old Corporation should cost $2000. Using the reinstating method, you will save hundreds of dollars. In Florida, you will pay $150 per year that the company missed its fees. If the company was incorporated in 1998 and it is now 2009 and the owners of the company stopped paying their fees in 2005, you first do all necessary checks to ensure the company is not in debt. After this is done you can now pay $600 for an 11-year-old corporation. Sounds like a deal? We will go into detail on how to find cheap shelf corporations, how to check the credit history of the corporation and how to acquire the corporation and build from that point. With this method, credit is acquired in much less time than if you were to build your corporate credit from the beginning. You have the choice as to how strong a company you will like to start with and this makes all the difference.

The process covered in this book can be done for every state that has a user-friendly secretary of state website. We have covered the state of Florida in this book. In order to apply this knowledge to other stats, you simple have to replace the "Finding of the corporation" section with the process that will apply to any other states that you will like to acquire corporations in.

This book is meant to take you to the next level in business credit building. It is a straight forward book that will give you all the tools you need to acquire business lines of credit in a very short space of time. I have done my very best to leave out all the fluff and unnecessary information. If you are not well versed in business credit building, I suggest that you read this book twice to educate yourself on business credit building. If you are reading this, you must understand that you have access to information and techniques of building business credit that 99% of the business world simply do not have access to. Most "business credit gurus" either do not know these techniques or will refuse to share them with you. I have chosen to divulge this information for two reasons; 1. Money is getting extremely scarce and business owners need this information more than ever; 2. I am moving away from business credit consulting and this book will fill that void. This book will take much of the waiting out of building business credit and take you straight to very high revolving lines of vendor credit as well as revolving cash credit. Let me break down the time line of acquiring corporate credit with "Unbreakable Laws of Business Credit" opposed to using the conventional method of building credit from the ground up. This book will teach you how to find a corporation, check the credit, and reinstate the corporation all in one day. The state takes 1-3 days to reinstate the corporation. Once the corporation is reinstated, you will have to contact D&B to change the basic contact information to the current contact information. i.e. The new business address, phone number and owner(s). This will take an additional 3-5 business days.

Now that D&B has updated the information, you are ready to rock and roll. You will immediately be able to apply for business credit lines depending on the strength of the corporation's credit. This book will literally take 6-8 months business credit building process and reduce it to 2 weeks. This book gives you the ability to actually become a shelf corporation vendor. With this book, you can literally establish hundreds of thousands of dollars in business credit using multiple corporations within a twelve-month period.

This book can eliminate the entire setting up and initial building process of the corporation. We will not completely rule out some of those initial net 30 accounts but we will now be able to get revolving lines of credit very early in the "game." We can now start with revolving accounts and move on and forgo those net 30 accounts.

Step 1: Go to your Secretary of State website and identify corporations that have been dissolved due to lack of payment to the state.

Step 2: Check the credit of the corporations that interest you. These are usually old corporations that have only been inactive for a short period. Identify the one you would like to obtain.

Step 3: Contact the current principal of the corporation and arrange for you to be the owner from that point on, if possible.

Step 4: Make the necessary preparations to reinstate the corporation. You will need to acquire a virtual office, a phone number and a registered agent for your corporation.

Step 5: Pay the states reinstatement fees and edit the address and officers to your new address (Your Home Address/Office Address/ Virtual Office Address)

Step 6: Call Dun and Bradstreet to get information updated. i.e. New Address, Officers, Phone Number, Resident Agent, etc. This usually takes about a week to be changed.

Step 7: Once all the information is changed you can start applying for credit. It's that simple.

The process of doing the initial research on a corporation was only described for the state of Florida in this book. This does not mean that it cannot be done for other states. I have done this process for a number of states and Florida's Secretary of State's is very user friendly. In order to acquire corporations in other states, you simply need to get very acquainted with their respective SOS website. See the "Elements Needed" section for a list of SOS websites.

Go to your Secretary of State Website to Research Corporations

Finding the Initial Corporations

What we are trying to do in this step is to find corporations that have gone out of business. We want old corporations that have recently gone inactive due to not paying state fees. The older the corporation, the more likely it is to have established credit. I am going through the techniques that I deem to be most efficient but you may find your own method. In my examples, we will be researching Florida corporations. Not only is Florida good for incorporating for tax purposes, but their Secretary of State website is the most user friendly I have seen. If you will like to research corporations in other states, you can go to your respective SOS website which is listed in the "Elements Needed" chapter.

Florida's SOS corporation website is www.sunbiz.org . You will first go to the Search Records on the top left-hand corner of their website. Then you go to "Inquire by name" section. I choose this option because this gives you a list of corporations

You are now brought to a search menu. You can search for one letter or a name. This will simple give you a list of corporations. You will also have the opportunity to go to the next page or go back a page to view more corporations.

After doing a search you can move forward and backward among company names, so in doing research you will start with a chosen search name and simply go through the list.

This is the "Status" of the corporation. ACT= active, INACT=inactive, INACT/UA=Inactive but unavailable. Strangely enough the corporations that we mainly want are the ones that say INACT/UA. The unavailable simply means that no one can currently incorporate another corporation with the same name because it has recently gone inactive. This is vital because in reinstating the corporations, we will be paying a certain fee per year of inactivity and these have the lowest inactive time. You can also research companies that are inactive but when you get experience, you will realize that you will come across many companies that have been inactive for more than ten years. By only using the INACT/UA corporations, this reduces the amount of research that you will have to do before you find a good corporation. This does not mean that I do not research INACT corporations as well, but I am just giving you the quickest method to success.

When looking for a corporation we must ensure that it is a "For Profit Corporation" or a "Limited Liability Corporation." This is an aspect that can easily be over looked.

Now that we have some insight on initially choosing a corporation to do research the status of INACT/UA.

The FEI/EIN Number:

This is the same as the Tax ID number. If the corporation does not have a Tax Id number, this will indicate that it has not had any credit activity. The next step is review date filed:

This is the incorporation date. I have found that corporations that are five years old and younger seldom have established credit files. I usually bypass these corporations and look for corporations incorporated in 2003 and before. If you are simply looking for aged corporations, this is not necessary but when strictly looking for corporations with an 80 paydex, you will want to stick to the older corporations. The final thing that you want to pay attention to is the Last Event.

This is the last event of the corporation with the state. You will be looking for corporations that read "REVOKED FOR ANNUAL REPORT" or "ADMIN DISSOLUTION FOR ANNUAL REPORT."

These are the only two situations where you can reinstate the corporation. Although we have found a company that was incorporated in 2004 and dissolved in 2008, we would not be able to reinstate this corporation even if, it has good credit. We have to continue looking until we find a corporation that meet all the criterias.

You want to continue searching for corporations that fit the criteria. When reviewing company profiles look for established EIN numbers that are more than five years old. Remember to pay attention to the last event or last activity.

Check the Credit of the Corporation

When you find an appropriate corporation, we have to check the credit of the corporation. D&B charges $40-$180 to check the credit of a corporation but we want to get the complete $180 credit file. Paying this fee is not cost effective since you may have to check the credit of multiple corporations before you find a good one. In order to get around this you will need to acquire a DnBi account from Dun&Bradstreet. DnBi is a service that D&B offers to corporations to check the credit of other corporations. We will cover the process of acquiring the account with no initial payment in the "Elements Needed" chapter. Choosing a corporation based on its credit is subjective. You may be looking for a corporation just for the age and you will do the credit building yourself, or you may be looking for a corporation with an 80 paydex or higher. I personally look for corporations with a 78+ paydex, with 5+ trades and one trade must be at least $500. When inspecting the credit file of any corporation, consider a number of key factors. These factors include a paydex of the corporation is 80, five trades and the largest trade must be a $1000 and under "Public Filings" there cannot be any judgments, liens, bankruptcies or lawsuits. I also make sure there is a phone number listed for the corporation. I have found that in about 70% of the cases, this number still works, and the old owner can usually be found by calling this number. There is also a section on the report under "Payment Details" and it should read "Now Owes."

Most of the time under "Business Registration" of the report, the company is listed as inactive. There are a number of ways to deal with this. You can fax in the active company charter to D&B once the company is reinstated. They will then change this on your company report. You must also note that some credit files do not have inactive listed on them. If you choose not to deal with D&B, you can leave this status as is. You may or may not have a problem with the lenders. If you do, you can simply fax the active company charter that can be found on your states "SOS" website to the lender who has the application and this will work. I have done this on many occasions. Now that we have thoroughly inspected the credit report, we can come to the conclusion that this is a company that we are interested in.

Contact the Previous Owner of the Corporation

This step is pretty straight forward, but in some cases may require some resourcefulness. Although the corporation is inactive, the previous owners have the right to the corporation. Some people who use this technique to acquire shelf corporations skip this step in some instances. At this stage, you will want to contact the listed principal of the corporation and let him know that you will like to acquire his corporation. You need to do this without making it apparent that the corporation has any "real" value. I usually start by calling the phone number listed on the corporation and asking for the listed CEO/President of the corporation. In most cases, the principal is at that phone number. Once I get into contact with the owner, I first confirm that he/she isn't doing business under the given name. Once this is confirmed you then have to continue to come to a strategic way of getting the corporation for "No Money" to them.

You can also let them know that the fees are at least $900 (which is true, but I will show you later in the book how to get around these fees).

You can even offer a couple hundred dollars for the owner's time for signing, but you must remember what you are getting out of this. Shelf corporations sell for thousands of dollars and this is saving you money. You can seek legal advice for more information on a potential contact for the sale of the corporation.

Finding the Contact Information

In a very few cases, there may not be a phone number listed on the D&B credit file; or the number on file may not work anymore. In these cases, there are only a few things that can be done. I usually go to http://www.whitepages.com to search for the owner's local phone number. If this is not successful I may simply search google for the name to see what I can find. This is a situation where you have to use your resourcefulness to find as much information as possible.

Prepare to Reinstate your New Corporation

Before you reinstate the corporation, you will need a number of factors in place:

1. Business Address

You will need this established before you reinstate the corporation because you will have to input this information when you reinstate the corporation. Your address can be a home address, an actual business address or a Virtual Office. A UPS store address is simply out of the question. I have used Regus.com for many of my virtual office needs, but they are very popular. In many cases, when using such a large virtual office provider, the lenders usually ask for a utility bill such as a phone bill to confirm that you are at that address. This can simply be avoided by choosing a smaller virtual office company. You can start your search by simply going to craigslist for any of the cities in the state that you are reinstating the corporation in and search for virtual offices.

2. Business Phone Number

One thing that I have noticed with these older corporations is that lenders are not as stringent with the 411 listing as they are for very young corporations, but in order to cover all bases, I still suggest you acquire a phone number that is listed in 411. When choosing a phone number, I will start with the number that is currently listed on the D&B file. If this number is out of service, I will contact the provider for that area (in Florida it is AT&T) and reactivate that phone number as an RCF (remote call forwarding number). This will do two things; it will reduce the amount of information that needs to be changed on the D&B file and it will allow you to be listed in 411. One option that you may want to consider is a Vumber number. You can get details at www.vumber.com. What this is, is a remote call forwarding number that you can return calls with. This is huge for some vendors that want you to return their calls.

3. Resident Agent

A registered agent is a business or individual designated to receive service of process (SOP) when a business entity is a party in a legal action such as a lawsuit or summons. Florida law (as do other states) requires each corporation to have a registered agent in the state. Many companies offer this service for $100 per year. One of these corporations can be found at http://www.incorp.com/florida-registered-agent.aspx. If you have a relative or friend who resides in the state of the corporation, they can act as the resident agent.

http://www.incorp.com/florida-registered-agent.aspxhttp://www.incorp.com/florida-registered-agent.aspxhttp://www.vumber.com/

Reinstate the Corporation

The reinstatement process is very simple for corporations that have been inactive for less than a year. i.e. Those that have a status of INACT/UA. Once you are on the profile page of the corporation, you can reinstate it online. First, click "Efiling Services," then "Reinstatement Filing."

Please not that if you are not working with a corporation that is not in the "INACT/UA" status, you can call 850-245-5069 to complete the process.

Once you get to the next page, everything is pretty much self-explanatory. You will have to change all necessary information to your new address, registered agent and principals. The one note at this point is the $600 reinstatement fee. I called the secretary of state to find out what are the requirements to waive the $600 fee and the rep stated, "Once you state that you did not get any notice, the fee will be waived."

Fix the Business Credit Files

Now that you have reinstated the corporation with the state, and changed the address and principals, you have to make the business credit bureaus aware of the changes to the corporation. There are a number of issues that we have to deal with at this point. It is important to note that you will not be able to contact Experian to have your credit file edited, you will have to wait until one of your new creditors report to Experian to establish a new credit file, but the good news is that your D&B file can easily be edited. We must first start by calling D&B at 1-800-234-3867, then choose "option 1" then "option 4". This is the department that will do the changes on the credit files. If you contact any other department they will be adamant about selling you one of their many products. When you are connected to a representative you must make them aware that you applied for credit and it was brought to your attention that your name is not on the credit file. You use this approach as a way of justifying your call to change the credit report. You must ensure that you do not mention that you recently purchased the corporation. If asked, you can say that you owned the corporation for 2-5 years. You are usually asked this when D&B calls back to verify the information. The change of ownership will not clear the credit file but under the "History and Operations" section on the credit report, the length of time that you have managed the corporation is stated. At this point, the only information that can be edited on the file is your name and the phone number listed on the corporation. Once you provide them with this information, the rep will inform you that you will be contacted in 3-7 business days to confirm the information. They will first check with the Secretary of State to ensure that the information provided is correct and then contact you to confirm the information provided. Once you have spoken to D&B again via phone it will take 24 hours for the information to be updated on the credit file. If at this stage, you have access to DnBi, you can follow the changes of the corporation online. If not, you will simply have to call back the 1-800 number provided above. At this point you are listed on the corporation and the phone number of the corporation was also changed. When you call back at this point, you will now change the address of the corporation to the one you have set up. Other than the address, this rep can also provide you with the E update login and password where you can change all other information such as the number of employees and the income. Before calling at this point you will need to ensure that you have an email set up for the corporation that is at hand. This will be necessary to acquire the e update username and password. It is important to note that any free email address will suffice. Many "gurus" claim that you will need your own domain name and custom email address. Although this may look better, it is definitely not necessary. Each time you change information on your credit file, it takes 3-7 days to be completed.

Apply for Credit

You are now at the point where your shelf corporation is set up correctly, D&B has the correct information and you are ready to roll with acquiring credit. If you have acquired a corporation with no established credit, you will have to start with net accounts. If you have acquired a corporation with an 80 paydex and it is more than two years old (which it should be) you will start with revolving accounts.

In order to accomplish everything in this book, you will need to have access to, and become very acquainted with three key elements.

1. The Secretary of State website of choice

2. DnBi. Yes, it's not a typo, there is an 'I' E update

The Secretary of State Website of Choice

Each state has a secretary of state website. This website usually encompasses services from elections to business incorporation for each state. In this book, we have covered using the Florida secretary of state website in detail. It can be found at www.sunbiz.org. This was done because in my opinion, this is a very simple website with many resources. Other SOS websites that have known to be simple are Nevada and Michigan. On the following page, you can view a table of the SOS websites for each state.

http://www.sunbiz.org/

Alabama www.sos. state.al.us

Alaska www.dced.state.ak.us/occ

Arizona http://www.azsos.gov/business_services/tnt/tnt_name_search_instructions.htm

Arkansas www.sosweb. state.ar .us/

California www.sos. ca .gov/business/

Colorado http://www.colorado.gov/

Connecticut www.ct.gov/sots/

Delaware http://sos.delaware.gov/

Florida www.sunbiz.org

Georgia sos.georgia .gov/

Idaho www.idsos. state.id.us/

Illinois http://www.cyberdriveillinois.com/

Indiana www.in.gov/sos

Iowa www.sos.state.ia.us/

Kansas www.kssos.org

Kentucky www.sos.ky.gov

Louisiana www.sos.louisiana.gov/

Maine www.maine.gov/sos/

Maryland www.sos.state.md.us/

Massachusetts www.sec.state.ma.us/

Michigan www.michigan.gov/sos

Minnesota www.sos.statemn.us/

Mississippi www.sos.state.ms.us/

Missouri www.sos.mo.gov/

Montana www.sos.mt.gov/

Nebraska www.sos.ne.gov

Nevada http://sos.state.nv.us/

New Hampshire www.sos.nh.gov

New Jersey www.state.nj.us/state

New Mexico www.sos.state.nm.us

New York www.dos.state.ny.us

North Carolina www.secretary.state.nc.us/corporations

North Dakota www.nd.gov/sos/businessserv

Ohio www.sos.state.oh.us

Oklahoma www.sos.state.ok.us/

Oregon www.sos.state.or.us/

Pennsylvania www.dos.state.pa.us/corps

Rhode Island www.state.ri.us

South Carolina www.scsos.com/

South Dakota www.sdsos.gov

Tennessee www.state.tn.us/sos

Texas www.sos.state.tx.us

Vermont www.sec.state.vt.us

Virginia www.scc.virginia.gov

Washington www.secstate.wa.gov

West Virginia www.wvsos.com

Wisconsin www.sos.state.wi.us

Wyoming soswy.state.wy.us

According to D&B, "DNBi is an interactive, customizable Web application that provides you with the most complete and up-to-date DUNS Right™ information available, as well as comprehensive monitoring and portfolio analysis. DNBi empowers you to make more informed, efficient, and insightful credit decisions by providing online access to the most complete and up-to-date information on over 120 million companies in the D&B global database." Basically, with DnBi you will be able to pull the D&B business credit files of various corporations (the corps that you will like to reinstate) as well as monitor their changes. In order to get a DnBi account you will first need a corporation.

If you do not have one at this point, do not fear, there is another way to check the credit, but DnBi is what you will really want to acquire.

Dealing with D&B is always a big aspect in this business credit industry so you need to understand how they work. In order to get a DnBi account at the best price you will want to call 1-800-234-3867.

This is D&B's DnBi contact number; you need to speak as if you previously spoke to someone so that much of the sales tactics will be reduced. Before you call D&B to establish an account, you must first understand how much DnBi costs and how it is billed in order to avoid being tricked by a rep. DnBi is usually charged per pull. D&B reps are allowed to charge anything above $20 per pull and you usually can start with a maximum of 250 pulls per year, which should bring the price down to around $22 per pull (you do not have to pay this upfront so do not fear). I have had situations where a rep tried to charge me $55 per pull which came up to $10,000+ per year. There is also an option to get unlimited pulls per year after your first year of using it. The cost of signing up is usually calculated by the year, so if it is agreed that you will like to get 250 pulls at $22 per pull, your yearly charge for the first year is $5500. Once you have come to an agreed price, the next step is negotiating payment terms. If your current corporation has any kind of credit what so ever (you do not even need a paydex score) you should be qualified to get the cost invoice into three payments paid at 30, 60 and 90 days. This is ideal because you do not have to come out of pocket right away for the service. I suggest trying to get these terms so that you can try the service and determine if you would like to keep it. If you choose not to and you do not pay D&B, they will simply report the lack of payment to your business credit report and your business credit will be no good anymore. If you do not have any established credit (usually meaning that you have nothing reporting) you can be billed on a monthly basis. In this situation where your yearly charge will be $5500, your monthly payment will now be $458.33 per month. This does not mean that you are limited to a number of pulls per month; this simply gives you the ability to spread the payments out. This is not the ideal situation, but it is well worth the money. Now that you understand the possible tricks of D&B with this service, let's get you ready to make the call. Do not feel obligated to take the first deal that a rep gives you. It may be beneficial to call back as all the reps are trying to make a commission. When I call DnBi, I usually explain that I spoke to someone a few days ago about a service called DnBi because I was thinking about extending credit to clients but I needed a system to check their business credit (I say this whether this is true or not. This reduces all the initial sales tactics). I then explain that I did not remember who I spoke to, but the rep explained that there are various payment options and prices for DnBi. I then claim that he mentioned something about having unlimited access as well as 250 pulls for around $5000 and I will like to get more information. Once you have stated all of this, the rep now has parameters to work within that you have given him. He will then go through the same payment options that I have mentioned above. You will want to try your very best to get it billed at that point. If the rep does not invoice you for the service, feel free to call back and tell the next rep that you spoke to a previous rep that told you that you will be able to be invoiced for the DnBi service, but you lost his contact information.

This rep will now do whatever it takes to get you the service that you requested at the terms that you stated. You may want to provide the rep with your email address where he can send you a number of potential options for the service. This will reduce the pressure for you to make an immediate decision and it will also give you more control over the situation.

After some negotiation (when necessary), you will now have access to DnBi, which is a very simple service. It is as simple to use a as search engine and this will bring you one step closer to acquiring multiple shelf corporations.

Checking Credit with Eupdate

This section is meant for informational purposes only. It is important that you keep track of your corporation as anyone can get access to a company's DnBi account. You first call D&B at 1-800-234-3867, then choose "option 1" then "option 4". Inform them that you would like to get access to your D&B account. They will ask you for the name of the principal (which is found on the profile of the company on the SOS website). You will also need an email address and the phone number of the corporation. Any email address will be fine, but you can search for the phone number of the corporation at www.manta.com, through 411 and yellowpages.com. If they ask for your DUNS number, you can simply say that you do not know it, but they can pull everything up with your business name, address and phone number.

Acquiring the shelf corporation is just the first step. After you acquire it, there are a couple hurdles you will need to overcome as well as processes that need to take place in order to maximize the use of your shelf corporation as well as all the future shelf corps that you will acquire. Some of the issues that we have to keep in mind are: 1. Doing Business in other states. i.e. your home state. 2. Where do you start when building business credit with a shelf corporation? 3. Waiting between applications. 4. Checking your Experian business credit file. 5 Potential issues that may arise with your shelf corporation.

Doing Business in Other States

If you do not reside in Florida, or whichever state you choose to acquire your shelf corporations, you will have some options of establishing an entity in order to do business in your home state. Many of my clients opt not to incorporate in their home state because it is an additional expense and it is not necessary. If you choose to simply keep the corporation in the initial state you simply will forward all mail and correspondence to yourself through your Virtual office. Please do not use USPS regular mail forwarding, this address will eventually show up on your D&B credit file as a mailing address.

If you would like to establish an entity in your home state with your shelf corporation, you will have file a "Foreign filing" in your state. This can be expensive as a Foreign Filing in Texas cost $700. It may be beneficial as your D&B file will now say that you have two locations and it will also save time and the hassle of forwarding all your mail. Many vendors also do not like to ship to other addresses other than your billing address. Dell in particular has known to close accounts after their initial order is to a different address other than the billing address.

Building business credit with your shelf corporation is a little different than building credit with a new corporation. If done right, your shelf corporation will already have a strong business credit file established, but this does not mean that you will be able to apply for every card known to man. One thing that we must note is that your Experian Business File cannot be updated as easily as your D&B file. When you change the owner and address on the corporation, if you apply to a vendor who pulls Experian Business he will not get any information available. This is due to the fact that there is no file established for your business at this new address. In order to deal with this, we must first apply to all the accounts that pull D&B. These are usually Citi accounts and GE Money usually pulls Experian Business. We must also note that when applying for credit, we do not want to go on a credit spree. This is not due to any potential inquiries as in personal credit, but this is simply due to the fact that most of the business credit accounts are not backed by the same banks; you do not want to apply for every Citi account available in the same week. The following is an example of my sequence of business credit applications once I have acquired a shelf corporation with a 78+paydex and it is now set up with the correct address, phone number and owner.

Day 1: Shelf corporation is corrected and ready to roll. Application 1 = Key Bank. Application 2 = Sears. Both of these applications are usually done on the first day that the corporation is ready.

Day 3: Call both Key Bank and Sears (Both backed by Citi) to find out if you are approved. They will also inform you that the card will be in the mail.

Day 10: Application 3 = Dell. This account is usually approved immediately online. Once this account is approved, do not order more than 5 personal computers at one time and stay away from ordering televisions in your early orders. This type of activity can raise red flags and has known to cause accounts to be closed. You may also place your first order when approved.

Day 15: Application 4 = Office Depot and Application 5 = Staples. These accounts are usually approved for $1500 - $4000 depending on how strong your corporation's credit is.

Please know that the accounts listed are not all the accounts that you are limited to applying to. I have just given my method of building business credit on these shelf corporations without raising red flags.

After I acquire these initial accounts (and any other Citi accounts, such as Exxon and Shell), I use them and wait 30-45 days after I make a payment for these accounts to now report to Experian. Once they report to Experian, I can now apply for all the GE Money accounts, such as Amazon, Sam's Discover, Walmart, etc. You can also view the various applications to get an idea which banks back which vendors.

Once you have paid the initial vendors and waited long enough, you will like to check your Experian business file. You will need to go to www.smartbusinesscreditreports.com and purchase one of their products. I suggest that you purchase one of their Business Credit Advantage Subscriptions plans as those are the most comprehensive files that they offer.

Overcoming Potential Problems

There are a number of potential problems that may arise when acquiring these shelf corporations and building credit on them. Some of them are: 1. The credit files being wiped. This is something that has been spoken about everywhere in the business credit arena. In order to avoid this, you must ensure that when you call to change the corporate information, and D&B returns your call to confirm the information, when asked how long you have owned this corporation, calmly say something like "since 2003." This will appear on your credit file.

There may be an "Inactive" note on your credit file. D&B, being who they are put an inactive note on some of the files and some of the files, they seem to have missed it. If this is the case you do not have to worry. Many lenders seem to overlook it, but you will not simply get denied for this. You may have to fax in the certificate of good standing, as mentioned previously.

Virtual office issues. I have noticed, when using those large virtual office names (never use UPS), the vendors may ask for a business license. This is simply to confirm that you do business at that address. In most cases, corporations do not need a business license to operate in Florida, so a utility bill will be fine. I usually fax in an AT&T bill.

Chapter 4

HOW TO GET A TAX ID NUMBER

After choosing how you will operate and filing the necessary paperwork, you should obtain a Federal Tax ID Number, also called an EIN or Employer Identification Number. You will need this number even if you do not establish a business credit profile because it is a necessary part of doing business. You can apply for an EIN number online at https://www.irs.gov.com. Once on the site, search for IRS Form SS-4. You can fill in the form online and receive an EIN in about 5-10 minutes.

You need a Tax ID Number for business credit, even if you don't have employees. You have to tie the Tax ID number with the Social Security number, so the IRS can identify an individual that belongs to that corporation. It can be any officer in your corporation, not only the chief owner or stockholder), but you do have to give a social security number, and if you are a one woman or one man show it probably has to be yours.

Does this affect your privacy? Not really, because the IRS does not divulge this information. Business owners are concerned not only with building their business credit, but asset protection and secrecy usually is a secondary concern. For instance, in Nevada you can hide as the owner of a corporation because you can get officers of the corporation other than yourself and even choose "nominees", professionals for hire that will put their names on your officers list from the state so that your identity will be hidden if anyone tried to sue your company. Another asset protection strategy is to have two corporations where one is the "holding company" for a corporation that owns another corporation. You do all your business activity in the subordinate corporation, and if one day someone sues, you will have your parent corporation or "holding company" place a lien or UCC-1 form on your corporation being sued. That way the financial assets of your corporation are already spoken for because they are attached by your other corporation. Some corporate officers like this method of asset protection and privacy.

However, the goal of privacy is the opposite of the goal of business credit. This is because when you are starting to build business credit you want the opposite of privacy. You want Dun & Bradstreet to come and visit your office as well as check your address and phone number. You want your bank to be able to reach you and verify that your business is located where you say it does, and you want both of them to be able to verify with your incorporating state that you exist as a Corporation, (or in the case of a sole proprietorship) that you exist as a business license in the city.

However, think of it this way, if you want business credit and are applying for the first time, think of a way that you can be public. It is very important to get a phone listing with "411" for your business. If you have an 800 number, get it listed with the telephone company. Get your number listed in the most legitimate form possible. If you are a very small business and always answer your own phone, you might spring about 25 dollars a month for 24-hour answering service that answers live, rather than a cheesy answering machine. If you are just starting a new corporation or LLC, and you need a tax ID number to start your business credit file, then go ahead and use your Social Security number. The reason is that although you may want to hide who you are once asset protection is the goal, when you are building business credit in the beginning you want to be public.

Your name needs to be on the officers list of the corporation. Does this mean that others can find you? Actually, if collectors or litigants mean to get a hold of you they will not be able to do it because the IRS does not release this information, namely whose social security number is associated with your corporation, Also, any officer can put their Social Security number on the Corporation and doesn't need to be the one that owns stock in the company. If you're just starting out, and there are no other officers of the Corporation (in other words you're a one-man show) and if you don't plan on getting sued in the near future then go-ahead and associate your social security number with the tax ID number. Can you put your 5-year-old niece on the?

Officer's list of your corporation? No, the officers of your corporation have to be 18 years or older.

Remember that the LLC holds the advantage, if someone wants to sue you personally and you have a corporate account, the prosecution can't touch it because it belongs to the corporation, which is a completely different entity. If you have someone that is trying to sue you as an LLC or corporation, you can use your asset protection corporation to place a lien on your corporation.

Business License

Every business is required to have a business license in order to operate a business within city and county limits. Be sure to check with your local city hall to find out the steps that need to be taken in order to obtain a business license.

Open a Corporate Checking and Savings Account in the Business Name

A business bank account reference is a part of the credit granting process for many creditors. Basically, they want to ensure that you are actually in business. With the highly competitive nature of the current banking industry, it should not be hard to find a bank where you can open a business account for as little as $100. As long as you research potential banks before you apply, you shouldn't have any problems. Some banking institutions offer free business checking with free online bill pay and other features as well. Inquire with your banking institution of choice regarding additional requirements in opening a business account. Please note that most banking institutions require an EIN, business license and incorporation status before opening an account. If your company is not incorporated the banks will not open a corporate bank account using your social security number and you never want to use your social security number.

SET-UP A Commercial Office

In order to maximize your chances of obtaining business credit, you need to establish a commercial business presence.

A commercial business presence includes:

- A telephone number listed in the local telephone directory in the name of the business.
- An office address in a commercial office location.

Establishing your business as a "commercial" instead of a home-based business will not only create the illusion to business credit grantor that your business is a viable one, but in verifying your business status by checking with the telephone company and validating the address you gave is zoned for business. Some low-cost alternatives to paying high commercial rents and telephone bills include:

Local Incubators

—Shared space small business offices usually sponsored and operated by local non-profits or city government agencies.

Virtual Offices

—Shared office space for small business usually operated by local office buildings.

Below you will find a few recommendations:

- HQ Global Workplace: http://www.hq.com
- Office Suites Plus: http://www.officesuitesplus.com

Virtual Phone Line

What is a virtual number? It is a telephone number outside of the physical area code you reside in and provided by telephone carriers and VoIP providers. It allows callers to make local calls from that area code to your phone. For example, if you live in Memphis and have a virtual phone number with a Los Angeles area code, anyone calling from Los Angeles is making a local call. There are many companies that offer virtual numbers with the area code that may live in or toll-free numbers.

uReach.com, Ringcentral.com, Onebox.com, Vonage.com, Earthlink.com and Magicjack.com are just a few. Be sure to do an internet search for the best virtual number for your company. If you decide to obtain a virtual number, you can go to www.listyourself. net to list your phone number in the 411 databases. Warning not all carriers will list your company so know that numbers from uReach does. This option will keep you from having to pay for a phone line to be installed in your home if you are running a homebased business. You can also set up a business remote call forwarding with companies such as AT&T and Pacific Bell.

Virtual fax numbers

Every company must have a separate fax number from their business phone line. A virtual fax number works great because there are no extra phone lines to install. With a virtual fax, you are issued a fax number that goes directly to your email account. Once you receive your fax via email you can print it out and it's just that simple. If it is a fax that needs to be signed, then you will need a fax machine to return the fax. You can always go to your local office supply store such as FedEx Kinkos to return a fax. We suggest that you eventually purchase a fax machine. Efax.com, Packetel.com, and Smartfax.com are great companies to establish fax numbers and send email to fax functions at a low monthly cost.

Chapter 5

DUN & BRADSTREET

Obtaining a Dun & Bradstreet Business Profile

If you are going to play with the big boys, and you want to get the largest low interest rate commercial loans for your business, then you must have a good rating with Dun&Bradstreet. Dun& Bradstreet, Experian and Equifax business are the three main companies that track business credit. There are others, but they are not as large or important. Experian is also not at all as large as Dun & Bradstreet. Dun & Bradstreet is 70% of the market share for business credit reporting and Experian is about 28% of the remaining.

Dun & Bradstreet is the important institution in tracking businesses, your DUNS number will make or break you in business credit. You need a DUNS number (a DUNS number is to a business what a social security number is to an individual) because it is your business identifying number for business credit. You can apply for a DUNS number on the Dun & Bradstreet website. If you do not plan on paying the $499 it can take up to 30 days to obtain your Dun & Bradstreet number. Now, if your company plans on applying for a government grant then you can receive your Dun & Bradstreet number in 48 hours. Apply for your D&B number at www.dnb.com

You want to get a Duns number and business profile by contacting Dun & Bradstreet on the phone or by email, but you want to be careful to make sure you are ready to talk to Dun & Bradstreet. The reason is that when they ask you what kind of business you are how many employees you have, etc.; you want to be careful what you want your business image to be; because once you give them information, it is very difficult to remove that information from your company profile.

For instance, if you tell them that you are a homebased business and you only have one employee, you are basically taking the risk of ruining your chances for having the highest type of business credit score. The one reserved for companies with 50 employees or more. Also, what you tell Dun & Bradstreet is put on the report and is permanent, so when you go to a bank to apply for a working capital loan or credit line, they may not like what is on your company credit report.

An example of what you want to tell Dun & Bradstreet in order to be eligible for the highest credit score (Paydex score of 75 or over. Will be explained in the next section get a Paydex score):

- Been in business 5 years.
- Gross more than a million in sales a year.
- 50 employees. (Some people go with 5 employees, but no less than 25 is necessary for a top credit score, i.e. 75 Paydex score)
- Business based in the same state as the officers of the company.
- Address and phone that is listed under your business name, phone that answers with your business name.
- A location that looks like an office, just in case a Dun & Bradstreet field officer shows up.
- More than one branch office, a headquarters office that you can be visited in, and a satellite office in another city. This can be accomplished by acquiring a virtual office space. Companies with more than one branch appear larger and more stable to Dun and Bradstreet.

Dun & Bradstreet will call to verify not only that your phone answers with your business name, but that you are listed and they will even go so far as to call the Secretary of State to verify that your company is really incorporated. Dun & Bradstreet will go through great lengths to protect their reputation by making sure you are honest in your business pursuits and that you really exist. As far as your financial statements, they rely on what you tell them for the most part, and you can state that you have 5-50 employees. Now, if your company plans on applying for a government grant then you can receive your Dun and Bradstreet number in 48 hours. Apply for your D&B number at www.dnb.com.

Tips on Applying for a DUNS Number

The first thing to understand about Duns and Bradstreet, is that you do not have to buy anything to receive a Paydex. Dun & Bradstreet will tell you otherwise but that is not true. The first thing to do is get D&B number and this can be done through three ways:

- First you can go online and get a number for free. It will take 30 days to get the number. It has been the experience of some people that didn't get a number after 30 days and after contacting D&B their response is the following: All they were applying for was a marketing number and you have to buy credit builder. This is not true.

- Second you can call 866-705-5711 and state you are applying for federal grants/contracts and you need a Duns number. They will give it to you on the spot with no solicitations.

- Finally, you can purchase credit builder which will include a Duns number and you also will get the number right away. Also, if you speak to a representative on the phone they sometimes give you the option of buying credit builder lite. This can be different prices as it is not listed on the website but others have paid $199 or $250 for it.

Once you receive your Duns number I would suggest whenever you apply for a net 30 or revolving account you include this number on your order form. Start with the credit building vendors like Uline, Viking, Nebs, and Staples. When you order and pay they will report to Dun & Bradstreet. This is how you will begin to build a credit file. If you purchase credit builder, then they should be adding vendors you have done business with in the past. This can include attorneys, accountants, utility/ telephone companies and anyone you have leased equipment or property.

Never supply your financial information if you do not plan on being consistent with updating each year. The reason why? Dun & Bradstreet is in the business of reselling information and once you provide your financial information; your competitors can go to their site and purchase a copy of your report including the financial record. For instance, you report one year because you had record profits and the following year you have record losses. Do you want to report those numbers too? What will the creditors think if you stop reporting because of a series of bad years? Not reporting once you have reported the financial information will raise a red flag and lower your business credit rating. If you feel you must post your financial information it is best to state that your sales are at least $2 million or more.

In order to help establish your business for longevity purposes, it is best to state that your business is at least 4-5 years old. It benefits your business profile. Keep in mind that even if you have recently incorporated the business, it is possible that you have been operating as a sole proprietorship prior to that point. In other words, it's a common occurrence to have a recent incorporation of a four- to five-year-old business.

DUNS Number

DUNS number stands for Data Universal Numbering System and it was introduced in 1963 to assign each company their own identifying nine-digit code. This is similar to your social security number or your company's employer identification number (EIN). The DUNS number is required by the Office of Budget and Management for any company applying for a grant with the government. For this reason, your company should be registered to be considered for government contracts and grants. After you have obtained your DUNS number you should register your company at the Central Contractor Registration (www.ccr.gov). The European Commission (the governing branch of the European Union), the Australian government, and the United Nations all use the DUNS number in their commercial dealings.

Paydex Scoring

A Paydex score is just like a personal credit score, but used for the purpose of obtaining business credit. It tells potential creditors about your payment history and commercial credit worthiness. The Paydex scores range from 0 to 100, with 100 being the best possible score. When building your Paydex score always try to maintain a score of 80 or above. The Paydex scoring model is as follows:

100- Pays before invoice is generated

90- Pays during discount period

80- Pays when invoice is due

70- Pays 15 days beyond terms

60- Pays 22 days beyond terms

50- Pays 30 days beyond terms

40- Pays 60 days beyond terms

20- Pays 90 days beyond terms

UN- Unavailable

Remember, in order to receive a Paydex score, you must have five tradelines reporting to Dun & Bradstreet. Once there are five tradelines reported, you will automatically be assigned a Paydex score. After you have been assigned a Paydex score you can begin to apply for revolving accounts and lines of credit.

Applying for Business Credit

The reason most companies cannot find funding is because they may not know where to look for the right funding source, how to pre-qualify before they apply, how to successfully present their request and not knowing how to apply.

Applying blindly is sending your deal to multiple lenders at the same time without pre-qualifying before you apply. Some lenders say NO because they don't do the type of funding you want or your deal doesn't meet their exact criteria. The rest say NO even though they would have done your deal, because no lender wants to be a third, fourth, or fifth in line. Remember creditors can be lazy. If your company name is Icon Management Inc. and a creditor does a search for your business and they enter Icon Management and nothing comes up they will deny your loan on the spot.

To be successful at applying for business credit you should know everything about the funding source's exact criteria for providing a loan. You should have a system that allows you to pre-qualify before you apply and you should have an accounts payable person. Before applying you should always know how much revenue your company makes or plans to make for the past and present fiscal year. Last always know the credit terms of the credit grantor.

Creditors will ask how much revenue your company generates. As a new company, you have not generated any revenue. Review your business plan or have strategic goals for your revenue. The goal is to make your company look as stable as possible.

Where to Apply for Business Credit

Below are lists of companies that will extend business credit immediately after your business has been established correctly. These companies can help you get the Paydex score that your company will need for future loans. Remember that patience is essential for building business credit. There are companies that will extend credit without having a Paydex score. If the application suggests a Dun & Bradstreet number and you have not obtained one, I suggest that you not apply until you get one. In order to open an account, some of the companies below will require you to purchase merchandise prior to opening a new account. Stay under $100 and the account will be opened without prepayment. In certain instances, a vendor may require that you prepay your order. If this happens proceed with prepayment so that the account can be opened and your payment history reported.

Reliable www.reliable.com (Make a purchase online or call and request a catalog)

Nebs www.nebs.com (Make a purchase online)

Staples www.staples.com (Make sure to fax a utility bill and business license with your application)

Uline www.uline.com (Decide on the items that you would, then give them a call and place your order. Remember to tell them you would like to set up an account.)

Interstate Battery www.ibsa.com (Click on 'my account' then click on "open a new business account.)

Once you have established these accounts always try and pay your invoices as soon as you receive them in the mail. The reason for this is because business creditors report timely payments and the sooner you pay the more you have a chance of increasing your Paydex score. If you need more supplies, it will be acceptable to place another order. The more orders that you place the more credit you are building. Once you have established your Paydex score of 80 or above the key is maintaining that level. The only way to keep your scores good is to pay your bills on time and make sure that you order from your suppliers once or twice a month.

Once you have received your Paydex score you can now apply to companies that sometimes require a DUNS number or a Paydex score.

The following pages contain a list of companies that extend credit to corporations and small business owner. Also listed are some terms that you should become familiar with if you are to be knowledgeable as it relates to business credit.

Revolving Credit: Allows you to carry a balance up to a pre-set limit and make monthly payments on the outstanding balance.

Net 30 Balance Due in full: The balance charged during the billing cycle must be paid in full within 30 days from the end of the billing cycle.

Net 30 Due (Monthly Billing): Accounts where there is a monthly recurring fee charged and 30 days from the date of the invoice.

National Pen Company
Telephone 866-900-7367 www.pens.com
No Personal Guarantee Required
They do not perform a Duns Number Check

ADP
Telephone 877-623-7729 www.adp.com
No Personal Guarantee Required
They do not perform a Duns Number Check

Advanta
Telephone 800-705-7255 www.advanta.com
Personal Guarantee Required
They do not perform a Duns Number Check

American Express
Telephone 800-519-6736 www.americanexperss.com
Personal Guarantee Required
They do not perform a Duns Number Check

Best Buy
Telephone 800-811-7276 www.bestbuy.com, www.bestbuybusiness.com
No Personal Guarantee Required
They do perform a Duns Number Check

Bill Me Later
Telephone 866-528-3733 www.billmelater.com
No Personal Guarantee Required
They do not perform a Duns Number Check

Books 2 Taxes
Telephone 888-897-4039
www.books2taxes.com
No Personal Guarantee Required
They do not perform a Duns Number Check

Capital One
Telephone 888-337-8562 www.capitalone.com
Personal Guarantee Required
They do not perform a Duns Number Check

Chase
Telephone 800-346-5838 www.chase.com
Personal Guarantee Required
They do not perform a Duns Number Check

Chevron-Texaco
Telephone 888-577-3355 www.chevrontexaco.com
Personal Guarantee Required
They do perform a Duns Number Check

Chrysler Financial
Telephone 800-556-8172
www.chryslerfinancial.com
Personal Guarantee Required
They do perform a Duns Number Check

Circle Lending
Telephone 800-805-2472
www.circlelending.com
No Personal Guarantee Required
They do not perform a Duns Number Check

Citi Business by Citibank
Telephone 877-528-0990
www.citibank.com
Personal Guarantee Required
They do not perform a Duns Number Check

CompUSA

Telephone 800-701-8431 www.compUSAbusiness.com
No Personal Guarantee Required
They do perform a Duns Number Check

Corporate Express

Telephone 888-238-6329 www.stablesadvantage.com
No Personal Guarantee Required
They do provide a Duns Number Check

Dell

Telephone 877-577-3355 www.dell.com
No Personal Guarantee Required
They do perform a Duns Number Check

DHL USA

Telephone 866-345-2329
www.dhl-usa.com
No Personal Guarantee Required
They do perform a Duns Number Check

Diner's Club

Telephone 800-438-3996 www.dinersclub.com
Personal Guarantee Required
They do perform a Duns Number Check

Direct Capital

Telephone 800-999-9942 www.directcapital.com
Personal Guarantee Required
They do perform a Duns Number Check

Discover

Telephone 888-347-2683 www.discover.com
Personal Guarantee Required
They do not perform a Duns Number Check

Exxon-Mobile

Telephone 800-438-3996
www.exxon.com
Personal Guarantee Required
They do perform a Duns Number Check

FedEx-Kinko's
Telephone 800-488-3705
www.fedex.com
No Personal Guarantee Required
They do perform a Duns Number Check

Ford Motor Credit
Telephone 800-567-6553 www.fordcredit.com
Personal Guarantee Required
They do perform a Duns Number Check

Fry's Electronics
Telephone 714-688-3000
www.frys.com
No Personal Guarantee Required
They do perform a Duns Number Check

General Motors Commercial financial
Telephone 800-327-6278
www.gmacfs.com
Personal Guarantee Required
They do perform a Duns Number Check

Grainger
Telephone 888-361-8649 www.grainger.com
No Personal Guarantee Required
They do perform a Duns Number Check

Home Depot
Telephone 800-685-6691 www.homedepot.com
No Personal Guarantee Required
They do perform a Duns Number Check

HP (Hewlett-Packard)
Telephone 888-277-5942
www.hp.com
No Personal Guarantee Required

JC Penney
Telephone 407-788-4022 www.jcpenney.com
No Personal Guarantee Required
They do perform a Duns Number Check

Lenovo (IBM)
Telephone 877-426-7624
www.lenovo.com
No Personal Guarantee Required
They do perform a Duns Number Check

Lowe's
Telephone 877-959-1007
www.lowes.com
No Personal Guarantee Required
They do perform a Duns Number Check

Macy's
Telephone 800-933-6229
www.macys.com
No Personal Guarantee Required
They do perform a Duns Number Check

National Capital Leasing
Telephone 866-615-6262 www.nationalcapitalleasing.com
Personal Guarantee Required
They do perform a Duns Number Check

Neiman Marcus
Telephone 800-685-6695 www.neimanmarcus.com
No Personal Guarantee Required
They do perform a Duns Number Check

New Egg
Telephone 800-390-1119 www.newegg.com
Personal Guarantee Required
They do not perform a Duns Number Check

Nordstrom's
Telephone 800-964-1800 www.nordstroms.com
No Personal Guarantee Required
They do perform a Duns Number Check

Oasis Outsourcing
Telephone 866-286-2747 www.oasisadvantage.com
No Personal Guarantee Required
They do not perform a Duns Number Check

Office Depot

Telephone 800-729-7744 www.officedepot.com
No Personal Guarantee Required

Office Furniture 2 Go

Telephone 800-460-0858 www.officefurniture2go.com
No Personal Guarantee Required
They do perform a Duns Number Check

Office Max

Telephone 877-633-4236 www.officemax.com
No Personal Guarantee Required
They do perform Duns Number Check

Orchard Supply

Telephone 408-281-3500
www.osh.com
No Personal Guarantee Required
They do perform a Duns Number Check

Paper Direct

Telephone 719-534-6251 www.paperdirect.com
No Personal Guarantee Required
They do not perform Duns Number Check

Paychex

Telephone 800-322-7292 www.paychex.com
No Personal Guarantee Required
They do not perform a Duns Number Check

Phillips 66

Telephone 800-648-4199 www.phillips66.com
No Personal Guarantee Required
They do perform a Duns Number Check

Pitney Bowes

Telephone 800-322-8000
www.pb.com
No Personal Guarantee Required
They do not perform a Duns Number Check

Prepaid Legal Services
Telephone 800-654-7757 www.prepaidlegal.com
No Personal Guarantee Required
They do not perform a Duns Number Check

Quill
Telephone 800-789-1331
www.quill.com
No Personal Guarantee Required
They do perform a Duns Number Check

Radio Shack
Telephone 888-773-2453 www.radioshack.com
No Personal Guarantee Required

Sam's Club
Telephone 888-746-7726 www.samsclubcredit.com
Personal Guarantee Required
They do not perform a Duns Number Check

SB Suite
Telephone 800-713-1282
www.sbsuite.com
No Personal Guarantee Required
They do not perform a Duns Number Check

Sears
Telephone 800-917-7700
www.sears.com
Personal Guarantee Required
They do not perform a Duns Number Check

Sinclair Oil
Telephone 800-340-3466 www.sinclairoil.com
Personal Guarantee Required
They do perform a Duns Number Check

Staples
Telephone 800-378-2753
www.staples.com
No Personal Guarantee Required
They do perform a Duns Number Check

Super fleet

Telephone 800-428-4016 www.superfleet.net
No Personal Guarantee Required
They do perform a Duns Number Check

TAD Accounting

Telephone 888-433-4737 www.tadaccounting.com
No Personal Guarantee Required
They do not perform a Duns Number Check

Tiger Direct

Telephone 866-311-0387 www.tigerdirect.com
Personal Guarantee Required
They do perform a Duns Number Check

Tiger leasing

Telephone 212-791-2250 www.tigerleasing.com
Personal Guarantee Required
They do perform a Duns Number Check

Uline

Telephone 800-958-5463
www.uline.com
No Personal Guarantee Required
They do perform Duns Number Check

Union 76

Telephone 800-944-7676 www.union76creditcard.com
No Personal Guarantee Required
They do perform a Duns Number Check

UPS

Telephone 800-742-5877
www.ups.com
No Personal Guarantee Required
They do perform a Duns Number Check

Wells Fargo Bank

Telephone 800-416-8658 www.wellsfargo.com
Personal Guarantee Required
They do not perform a Duns Number Check

Wholesale Janitorial Supply
Telephone 800-908-1986 www.wholesalejanitorialsupply.com
No Personal Guarantee Required
They do perform a Duns Number Check

Wright Express Fleet Card
Telephone 800-395-0812 www.wrightexpress.com
Personal Guarantee Required
They do perform a Duns Number Check

Amazon.com
www.amazon.com

American Needle
www.americanneedle.com

Arco
www.arco.com

Barnes & Noble
www.barnesnoble.com
(Apply under purchase order account)

Borders
www.borders.com

Citgo fleet
www.citgo.com

Conoco/Phillips 66/76
www.conoco.com

Deluxe
www.deluxe.com

Gemplers
www.gemplers.com

HD Expo
www.expo.com

Home Depot Master Card
www.homedepot.com/cards

Marathon

www.marathon.com

Nextel

www.nextel.com

Northern Tools

www.northerntool.com

Perazzi Apparel

www.perazziapparel.com

Savannah Suites

www.savannahsuites.com

Shell fleet

www.shell.com

Sprint

www.sprint.com

Sunoco Corporate

www.sunoco.com

Rapid forms

www.rapidforms.com

Rapid fuel

www.rapidfuel.com

T-Mobile

www.t-mobile.com

Target

www.target.com

Toys R Us

www2.toysrus.com/guest/corpsales.cfm
Valero www.valero.com

Business-Friendly Creditors List

Vendor ADP
Vendor Type Payroll & HR services
Personal Guarantee Required   **Automatically Reports to DNB?** ✓
Performs a Duns Number Check   **Automatically Reports to Experian**
Paydex Score Required
Terms Net 30 due (monthly billing)
Other Requirements Reports to DNB when verified by DNB. Call for additional terms.
How to Apply Telephone, website
Telephone 877-623-7729
Website www.adp.com

Vendor Advanta
Vendor Type Business credit cards
Personal Guarantee Required ✓   **Automatically Reports to DNB**
Performs a Duns Number Check   **Automatically Reports to Experian**
Paydex Score Required
Terms Revolving
Other Requirements Good personal credit. Outstanding balance does not appear on personal credit reports.
How to Apply Website
Telephone 800-705-7255
Website www.advanta.com

Vendor American Express
Vendor Type Business credit cards
Personal Guarantee Required?   **Automatically Reports to DNB**
Performs a Duns Number Check?   **Automatically Reports to Experian**
Paydex Score Required
Terms Revolving and Net 30 Due in Full accounts
Other Requirements Excellent personal credit. Outstanding balance does not appear on personal credit reports.
How to Apply Website
Telephone 800-519-6736
Website www.americanexpress.com

Vendor   Best Buy
Vendor Type   Electronics
Personal Guarantee Required   **Automatically Reports to DNB** ✓
Performs a Duns Number Check? ✓   **Automatically Reports to Experian**
Paydex Score Required ✓
Terms   Revolving
Other Requirements Call for other requirements.
How to Apply   Website, store
Telephone   800-811-7276
Website   www.bestbuy.com

Vendor   Bill Me Later
Vendor Type   Business & fleet gas card
Personal Guarantee Required   **Automatically Reports to DNB**
Performs a Duns Number Check   **Automatically Reports to Experian**
Paydex Score Required
Terms   No payments for 90 days or 6 months depending on the
                      participating merchant.
Other Requirements Visit the website for the list of 100+ merchants and
                      additional terms.
How to Apply   Website
Telephone   866-528-3733
Website   www.billmelater.com

Vendor   Books 2 Taxes
Vendor Type   Accounting & bookkeeping services
Personal Guarantee Required   **Automatically Reports to DNB** ✓
Performs a Duns Number Check   **Automatically Reports to Experian**
Paydex Score Required
Terms   Net 30 due (monthly billing)
Other Requirements Reports to DNB when verified by DNB. Call for additional
                      terms.
How to Apply   Website, telephone
Telephone   888-897-4039
Website   www.books2taxes.com

Vendor Capital One
Vendor Type Business credit card
Personal Guarantee Required? ✓   **Automatically Reports to DNB**
Performs a Duns Number Check   **Automatically Reports to Experian**
Paydex Score Required
Terms Revolving
Other Requirements Excellent personal credit. Outstanding balance does not appear on personal credit reports.
How to Apply Website
Telephone 888-337-8562
Website www.capitalone.com

Vendor Chase
Vendor Type Business credit card
Personal Guarantee Required ✓   **Automatically Reports to DNB**
Performs a Duns Number Check   **Automatically Reports to Experian**
Paydex Score Required
Terms Revolving
Other Requirements Good personal credit. Outstanding balance does not appear on personal credit reports.
How to Apply Website/Branch
Telephone 800-346-5838
Website www.chase.com

Vendor Chevron-Texaco
Vendor Type Business & fleet gas card
Personal Guarantee Required ✓   **Automatically Reports to DNB** ✓
Performs a Duns Number Check ✓   **Automatically Reports to Experian**
Paydex Score Required
Terms Revolving and net 30 due in full accounts
Other Requirements Minimum 2 years in business; if DUNS Number is not available, provide 2 trade references.
How to Apply Website, store
Telephone 888-577-3355
Website www.chevrontexaco.com

Vendor   Chrysler Financial
Vendor Type   Vehicle leasing, auto loans & commercial financing
Personal Guarantee Required ✓   **Automatically Reports to DNB?** ✓
Performs a Duns Number Check ✓   **Automatically Reports to Experian?** ✓
Paydex Score Required ✓
Terms   Various financing options
Other Requirements Visit the website or call for terms.
How to Apply   Website
Telephone   800-556-8172
Website   www.chryslerfinancial.com

Vendor   Circle Lending (Now "VIRGINMONEYUS")
Vendor Type   Person-to-person lending management
Personal Guarantee Required   **Automatically Reports to DNB** ✓
Performs a Duns Number Check   **Automatically Reports to Experian**
Paydex Score Required
Terms   Person-to-business and person-to-person loans.
Other Requirements Visit the website for details.
How to Apply   Website
Telephone   800-805-2472
Website   www.virginmoneyus.com

Vendor   Citi Business by Citibank
Vendor Type   Business credit card
Personal Guarantee Required ✓   **Automatically Reports to DNB**
Performs a Duns Number Check   **Automatically Reports to Experian**
Paydex Score Required
Terms   Revolving
Other Requirements Good personal credit. Outstanding balance does not
                        appear on personal credit reports.
How to Apply   Website, telephone
Telephone   877-528-0990
Website   www.citibank.com

Vendor   CompUSA

Vendor Type   Computers, peripherals & electronics

Personal Guarantee Required?   **Automatically Reports to DNB?** ✓

Performs a Duns Number Check? ✓   **Automatically Reports to Experian**

Paydex Score Required

Terms   Revolving and Net 30 balance due in full.

Other Requirements Call for details.

How to Apply   Telephone, website

Telephone   800-701-8431

Website   www.compUSAbusiness.com

Vendor   Corporate Express

Vendor Type   Office furniture & equipment.

Personal Guarantee Required   **Automatically Reports to DNB** ✓

Performs a Duns Number Check   **Automatically Reports to Experian**

Paydex Score Required

Terms   Revolving and Net 30 balance due in full accounts

Other Requirements You must call or visit the website to request a credit application package.

How to Apply   Telephone, online

Telephone   888-238-6329

Website www.cexp.com

Vendor   Dell

Vendor Type   Computers, peripherals & electronics

Personal Guarantee Required   **Automatically Reports to DNB** ✓

Performs a Duns Number Check ✓   **Automatically Reports to Experian?**

Paydex Score Required

Terms   Revolving net 30 or revolving

Other Requirements Minimum 2 years in business; provides either commercial or business credit account.

How to Apply Website

Telephone   877-577-3355

Website   www.dell.com

Vendor   Diner's Club
Vendor Type   Business credit card
Personal Guarantee Required? ✓   **Automatically Reports to DNB** ✓
Performs a Duns Number Check? ✓   **Automatically Reports to Experian?**
Paydex Score Required?
Terms   Revolving
Other Requirements $200k net worth; each cardholder provides a personal guarantee.
How to Apply   Website, telephone
Telephone   800-438-3996
Website   www.dinersclub.com

Vendor   Direct Capital
Vendor Type   Equipment leasing
Personal Guarantee Required   **Automatically Reports to DNB?** ✓
Performs a Duns Number Check   **Automatically Reports to Experian**
Paydex Score Required
Terms   Installment
Other Requirements 2 trade references; 1 bank reference; 1 vendor reference; you can also apply by fax at 603-766-8453.
How to Apply   Website, telephone
Telephone   800-999-9942
Website   www.directcapital.com

Vendor   Discover
Vendor Type   Business credit card
Personal Guarantee Required   **Automatically Reports to DNB?**
Performs a Duns Number Check?   **Automatically Reports to Experian?**
Paydex Score Required?
Terms   Revolving
Other Requirements Good personal credit. Outstanding balance does not appear on personal credit reports.
How to Apply Website, telephone
Telephone   888-347-2683
Website   www.discover.com

Vendor	Exxon-Mobil
Vendor Type	Business & fleet gas card
Personal Guarantee Required	**Automatically Reports to DNB** ✓
Performs a Duns Number Check	**Automatically Reports to Experian**
Paydex Score Required	
Terms	Net 30 balance due in full
Other Requirements	Minimum 3 years in business; 1-year secured account if the business is < 3 years old.
How to Apply	Website, store
Telephone	800-438-3996
Website	www.exxon.com

Vendor	FedEx
Vendor Type	Mail & printing services
Personal Guarantee Required	**Automatically Reports to DNB** ✓
Performs a Duns Number Check	**Automatically Reports to Experian**
Paydex Score Required	
Terms	Net 30 balance due in full
Other Requirements	A DUNS Number is the only requirement to open a business account
How to Apply	Website, in store
Telephone	800-488-3705
Website	www.fedex.com

Vendor	Ford Motor Credit
Vendor Type	Vehicle leasing, auto loans & commercial financing
Personal Guarantee Required	**Automatically Reports to DNB** ✓
Performs a Duns Number Check	**Automatically Reports to Experian**
Paydex Score Required	
Terms	Various financing options
Other Requirements	Visit the website or cad for terms.
How to Apply	Website
Telephone	800-567-6553
Website	www.fordcredit.com

106

Vendor   Fry's Electronics
Vendor Type   Computers, Peripherals & Electronics
Personal Guarantee Required?   **Automatically Reports to DNB** ✓
Performs a Duns Number Check   **Automatically Reports to Experian**
Paydex Score Required
Terms   Net 30 balance due in full
Other Requirements 3 trade references; 1 bank reference; financials and
                    balance sheet required; credit card cannot be used for online
                    purchases.
How to Apply   Telephone
Telephone   714-688-3000
Website   www.frvs.com

Vendor   General Motors Commercial Financial
Vendor Type   Vehicle leasing, Auto Loans & Commercial Financing
Personal Guarantee Required   **Automatically Reports to DNB** ✓
Performs a Duns Number Check   **Automatically Reports to Experian**
Paydex Score Required
Terms   Various financing options
Other Requirements Visit website or call for application and terms. Fleet
                    Financing: 800-353-3867.
How to Apply   Website, telephone
Telephone   800-327-6278
Website   www.qmacfs.com

Vendor   Grainger
Vendor Type   Business & office supplies
Personal Guarantee Required   **Automatically Reports to DNB** ✓
Performs a Duns Number Check   **Automatically Reports to Experian**
Paydex Score Required
Terms   Net 30 balance due in full
Other Requirements 3 trade references with 3-months of recent activity; 1-2
                    bank references.
How to Apply Website
Telephone   888-361-8649
Website   www.arainaer.com

Vendor   Home Depot
Vendor Type   Building supplies
Personal Guarantee Required   **Automatically Reports to DNB** ✓
Performs a Duns Number Check Automatically Reports to Experian
Paydex Score Required
Terms   Revolving
Other Requirements $2 million in sales or 10 employees or minimum 2 years in business to avoid providing a personal guarantee.
How to Apply Website, in store
Telephone   800-685-6691
Website   www.homedepot.com

Vendor   HP (Hewlett-Packard)
Vendor Type   PCs, printers & peripherals
Personal Guarantee Required   **Automatically Reports to DNB** ✓
Performs a Duns Number Check Automatically Reports to Experian
Paydex Score Required
Terms   Up to 60 months financing; equipment leasing
Other Requirements Call for additional **terms.**
How to Apply   **Telephone, website**
Telephone   888-277-5942
Website   www.hp.com

Vendor   JC Penney
Vendor Type   Clothing & accessories
Personal Guarantee Required   **Automatically Reports to DNB** ✓
Performs a Duns Number Check   **Automatically Reports to Experian**
Paydex Score Required
Terms   Net 30 balance due in full
Other Requirements Reports to DNB by request. Minimum 6 months in business.
How to Apply Telephone
Telephone   407-788-4022
Website   www.jcpenney.com

Vendor Lenovo (IBM)
Vendor Type PCs, printers & peripherals
Personal Guarantee Required **Automatically Reports to DNB** ✓
Performs a Duns Number Check **Automatically Reports to Experian**
Paydex Score Required
Terms Up to 60 months financing; 24-month leases
Other Requirements Call for additional **terms**.
How to Apply Telephone, website
Telephone 877-426-7624
Website www.lenovo.com

Vendor Lowe's
Vendor Type Building supplies
Personal Guarantee Required **Automatically Reports to DNB** ✓
Performs a Duns Number Check **Automatically Reports to Experian**
Paydex Score Required
Terms Revolving net 30
Other Requirements No personal guarantee is required if the business is
3 years old.
How to Apply Website, in store
Telephone 877-959-1007
Website www.lowes.com

Vendor Macy's
Vendor Type Clothing & accessories
Personal Guarantee Required **Automatically Reports to DNB** ✓
Performs a Duns Number Check **Automatically Reports to Experian?**
Paydex Score Required
Terms Net 30 balance due in full
Other Requirements Minimum of 2 years in business; 2-3 trade references;
1-2 bank references.
How to Apply Telephone
Telephone 800-933-6229
Website www.macys.com

Vendor   Meridian Capital Partners
Vendor Type   Equipment leasing & financing
Personal Guarantee Required   **Automatically Reports to DNB**
Performs a Duns Number Check   **Automatically Reports to Experian**
Paydex Score Required
Terms $1 buyout; term leases; other.
Other Requirements Meridian has "C" credit (bad credit) leasing programs and a one page application process up to $100,000. The company also has several other financing programs and alternatives.
How to Apply Website; telephone
Telephone   504-342-4912
Website   www.MCPFunding.com

National Pen Company Business promotional items
Vendor Vendor Type
Personal Guarantee Required   **Automatically Reports to DNB**
Performs a Duns Number Check   **Automatically Reports to Experian**
Paydex Score Required
Terms   Balance due upon receipt of the order
Other Requirements Call for credit approval.
How to Apply   Website
Telephone   866-900-7367
Website   www.pens.com

Vendor   Neiman Marcus
Vendor Type   Clothing & accessories
Personal Guarantee Required   **Automatically Reports to DNB** ✓
Performs a Duns Number Check   **Automatically Reports to Experian**
Paydex Score Required
Terms   Net 30 balance due in full
Other Requirements Must be in business at least 2 years to avoid providing a personal guarantee.
How to Apply Telephone
Telephone   800-685-6695
Website   www.neimanmarcus.com

Vendor   New Egg
Vendor Type   PCs, printers, peripherals & electronics
Personal Guarantee Required   **Automatically Reports to DNB** ✓
Performs a Duns Number Check   **Automatically Reports to Experian**
Paydex Score Required
Terms   Revolving
Other Requirements Reports to DNB by request. Minimum purchase of $500
                      required; no payments for 6 months.
How to Apply Website
Telephone   800-390-1119
Website   www.newegg.com

Vendor   Nordstrom's
Vendor Type   Clothing & accessories
Personal Guarantee Required   **Automatically Reports to DNB** ✓
Performs a Duns Number Check   **Automatically Reports to Experian**
Paydex Score Required
Terms   Net 30 balance due in full
Other Requirements 3-4 existing trade references; 2 trades should be Net 30
                      due accounts.
How to Apply Telephone
Telephone   800-964-1800
Website   www.nordstroms.com

Vendor   Oasis Outsourcing
Vendor Type   HR, employee benefits & risk management
Personal Guarantee Required   **Automatically Reports to DNB** ✓
Performs a Duns Number Check   **Automatically Reports to Experian**
Paydex Score Required
Terms   Net 30 due (monthly billing)
Other Requirements Reports to DNB when verified by DNB. Call for additional
                      terms.
How to Apply   Website
Telephone   866-286-2747
Website   www.oasisadvantage.com

Vendor   Office Depot
Vendor Type   Business & office supplies
Personal Guarantee Required   **Automatically Reports to DNB** ✓
Performs a Duns Number Check   **Automatically Reports to Experian**
Paydex Score Required
Terms   Revolving
Other Requirements Must be a corporation or LLC; minimum $1 million in sales if the business is 2 years old.
How to Apply **Website**, in store
Telephone   800-729-7744
Website   www.officedepot.com

Vendor   Office Furniture 2 Go
Vendor Type   Office furniture
Personal Guarantee Required   **Automatically Reports to DNB**
Performs a Duns Number Check   **Automatically Reports to Experian**
Paydex Score Required
Terms   Net 30 balance due in full
Other Requirements Call for details.
How to Apply **Telephone**
Telephone   800-460-0858
Website   www.officefurniture2go.com

Vendor   Office Max
Vendor Type   Business & office supplies
Personal Guarantee Required   **Automatically Reports to DNB** ✓
Performs a Duns Number Check   **Automatically Reports to Experian**
Paydex Score Required
Terms   Revolving net 30
Other Requirements Minimum 2 years in business; personal guarantee required if the business is < 2 years old.
How to Apply **Website**, in store
Telephone   877-633-4236
Website   www.officemax.com

Vendor   Orchard Supply
Vendor Type   Building supplies
Personal Guarantee Required   **Automatically Reports to DNB** ✓
Performs a Duns Number Check   **Automatically Reports to Experian**
Paydex Score Required
Terms   Revolving net 30
Other Requirements 3 trade references with 3 months of recent activity;
                      1-2 bank references.
How to Apply Website
Telephone   408-281-3500
Website   www.osh.com

Vendor   Paper Direct
Vendor Type   Stationary & promotional supplies
Personal Guarantee Required   **Automatically Reports to DNB** ✓
Performs a Duns Number Check   **Automatically Reports to Experian**
Paydex Score Required
Terms   Net 30 due.
Other Requirements 1 bank; 3 trade references.
How to Apply Telephone
Telephone   719-534-6251
Website   www.paperdirect.com

Vendor   Paychex
Vendor Type   Payroll & HR services
Personal Guarantee Required   **Automatically Reports to DNB** ✓
Performs a Duns Number Check   **Automatically Reports to Experian**
Paydex Score Required
Terms   Net 30 due (monthly billing)
Other Requirements Reports to DNB when verified by DNB. Call for additional
                      terms.
How to Apply Website, telephone
Telephone   800-322-7292
Website   www.pavchex.com

Vendor   Phillips 66
Vendor Type   Business & fleet gas card
Personal Guarantee Required   **Automatically Reports to DNB** ✓
Performs a Duns Number Check   **Automatically Reports to Experian**
Paydex Score Required
Terms   Net 30 due in full
Other Requirements Minimum 2 years in business.
How to Apply Website, in store
Telephone   800-648-4199
Website   www.phillips66.com

Vendor   Pitney Bowes
Vendor Type   Business mailing processing solutions
Personal Guarantee Required   **Automatically Reports to DNB** ✓
Performs a Duns Number Check   **Automatically Reports to Experian**
Paydex Score Required
Terms   Net 30 balance due in full
Other Requirements Call for additional terms.
How to Apply Website
Telephone   800-322-8000
Website www.pb.com

Vendor   Prepaid Legal Services
Vendor Type   Legal representation
Personal Guarantee Required   **Automatically Reports to DNB**✓
Performs a Duns Number Check   **Automatically Reports to Experian**
Paydex Score Required
Terms   Net 30 due (monthly billing)
Other Requirements Call for additional terms. Request information on small
                business representation. Reports to DNB when verified by
                DNB.
How to Apply Telephone
Telephone   800-654-7757
Website www.prepaidlegal.com

Vendor   Quill
Vendor Type   Business & office supplies
Personal Guarantee Required   **Automatically Reports to DNB**✓
Performs a Duns Number Check   **Automatically Reports to Experian**
Paydex Score Required
Terms   Net 30 balance due in full
Other Requirements
How to Apply Telephone
Telephone   800-789-1331
Website   www.quill.com

Vendor   Radio Shack
Vendor Type   Electronics
Personal Guarantee Required   **Automatically Reports to DNB** ✓
Performs a Duns Number Check   **Automatically Reports to Experian**
Paydex Score Required
Terms   Net 30 balance due in full
Other Requirements Personal guarantee required for partnerships and sole
          proprietorships.
How to Apply Website
Telephone   888-773-2453
Website   www.radioshack.com

Vendor   Sam's Club
Vendor Type   Wholesale goods
Personal Guarantee Required   **Automatically Reports to DNB**
Performs a Duns Number Check   **Automatically Reports to Experian**
Paydex Score Required
Terms   Revolving
Other Requirements Visit the website for additional terms. Sam's Club also has
          a $100k line of credit product for businesses.
How to Apply Website, in store
Telephone   888-746-7726
Website   www.samsclubcredit.com

Vendor SB Suite
Vendor Type Accounting & bookkeeping services
Personal Guarantee Required? **Automatically Reports to DNB?** ✓
Performs a Duns Number Check? **Automatically Reports to Experian?**
Paydex Score Required?
Terms Net 30 due (monthly billing)
Other Requirements Reports to DNB when verified by DNB. Call for additional
terms.
How to Apply Website, telephone
Telephone 800-713-1282
Website www.sbsuite.com

Vendor Sears
Vendor Type Building supplies
Personal Guarantee Required? ✓ **Automatically Reports to DNB?** ✓
Performs a Duns Number Check? **Automatically Reports to Experian?**
Paydex Score Required?
Terms Revolving
Other Requirements Personal guarantee required if the business is < 2 years old.
How to Apply Website, in store
Telephone 800-917-7700
Website www.sears.com

Vendor Sinclair Oil
Vendor Type Business & fleet gas card
Personal Guarantee Required **Automatically Reports to DNB** ✓
Performs a Duns Number Check **Automatically Reports to Experian**
Payed Score Required
Terms Net 30 balance due in full
Other Requirements 4 trade references; each cardholder provides a personal
guarantee.
How to Apply Website
Telephone 800-340-3466
Website www.sinclairoil.com

Vendor   Staples
Vendor Type   Business & office supplies
Personal Guarantee Required   **Automatically Reports to DNB** ✓
Performs a Duns Number Check   **Automatically Reports to Experian**
Paydex Score Required?
Terms   Revolving or Net 30 balance due in full
Other Requirements Minimum 2 years in business.
How to Apply   Website, in store
Telephone   800-378-2753
Website   www.staples.com

Vendor   Super fleet
Vendor Type   Business & fleet gas card
Personal Guarantee Required   **Automatically Reports to DNB** ✓
Performs a Duns Number Check   **Automatically Reports to Experian**
Paydex Score Required
Terms   Net 30 balance due in full
Other Requirements Minimum 1 year in business.
How to Apply   Website
Telephone   800-428-4016
Website   www.superfleet.net

Vendor   TAD Accounting
Vendor Type   Accounting & bookkeeping services
Personal Guarantee Required   **Automatically Reports to DNB** ✓
Performs a Duns Number Check   **Automatically Reports to Experian**
Paydex Score Required
Terms   Net 30 due (monthly billing)
Other Requirements Reports to DNB when verified by DNB. Call for additional
                      terms.
How to Apply   Website, telephone
Telephone   888-433-4737
Website   www.tadaccounting.com

Vendor   Tiger Direct
Vendor Type   Computers, peripherals & electronics
Personal Guarantee Required   **Automatically Reports to DNB** ✓
Performs a Duns Number Check   **Automatically Reports to Experian**
Paydex Score Required
Terms   Net 30 balance due in full
Other Requirements Standard Industrial Classification (SIC) code required; 3
                    trade references and bank reference required.
How to Apply Website
Telephone   866-311-0387
Website   www.tigerdirect.com

Vendor   Tiger Leasing
Vendor Type   Equipment leasing
Personal Guarantee Required ✓   **Automatically Reports to DNB** ✓
Performs a Duns Number Check ✓   **Automatically Reports to Experian**
Paydex Score Required
Terms   Installment lease
Other Requirements 1 -2 bank references; 3 trade references.
How to Apply   **Website, telephone**
Telephone   212-791-2250
Website www.tigerleasing.com

Vendor   Uline
Vendor Type   Janitorial supplies
Personal Guarantee Required   **Automatically Reports to DNB** ✓
Performs a Duns Number Check   **Automatically Reports to Experian**
Paydex Score Required
Terms   Net 30 balance due in full
Other Requirements 1 -2 trade references.
How to Apply   Website
Telephone   800-958-5463
Website   www.uline.com

Vendor   Union 76
Vendor Type   Business & fleet gas card
Personal Guarantee Required   **Automatically Reports to DNB** ✓
Performs a Duns Number Check   **Automatically Reports to Experian**
Paydex Score Required

Terms   Revolving; net 30 balance due in full

Other Requirements 2-3 trade references; 1-2 bank references.

How to Apply   Website, in store

Telephone   800-944-7376

Website   www.union76creditcard.com

Vendor   UPS

Vendor Type   Packaging & shipping

Personal Guarantee Required   **Automatically Reports to DNB** ✓

Performs a Duns Number-Check   **Automatically Reports to Experian**

Paydex Score Required

Terms   Net 30 full balance due with a Paydex Score.

Other Requirements Net 7 full balance due invoiced weekly if automatically
                     billed to a credit card.

How to Apply   Website

Telephone   800-742-5877

Website   www.ups.com

Vendor   Wells Fargo Bank

Vendor Type   Business credit card

Personal Guarantee Required   **Automatically Reports to DNB**

Performs a Duns Number Check   **Automatically Reports to Experian**

Paydex Score Required

Terms   Business secured MasterCard to $50,000; revolving account.

Other Requirements Outstanding balance does not appear on your personal
                     credit reports.

How to Apply Website

Telephone   800-416-8658

Website   www.wellsfargo.com

Vendor   Wholesale Janitorial Supply
Vendor Type   Janitorial supplies
Personal Guarantee Required   **Automatically Reports to DNB** ✓
Performs a Duns Number Check   **Automatically Reports to Experian**
Paydex Score Required
Terms   Net 30 balance due in full
Other Requirements 2 trade reference; 1 bank reference; valid credit card (visa, MasterCard, discover, American Express).
How to Apply   Website
Telephone   800-908-1986
Website   www.wholesalejanitorialsupplv.com

Vendor   Wright Express Fleet Card
Vendor Type   Business & fleet gas card
Personal Guarantee Required   **Automatically Reports to DNB**∨
Performs a Duns Number Check   **Automatically Reports to Experian**
Paydex Score Required
Terms   Net 26 balance due in full
Other Requirements Minimum 3 years in business; no personal guarantee required if the business is 3 years old.
How to Apply   Website, in store
Telephone   800-395-0812
Website   www.wrightexpress.com

Resources

Internet Resources

1 800-flowers.com
http://ww2.1800flowers.com/flowers/corporate/benefits.asp

3M Company
http://solutions.3m.com/wps/portal/!ut...VAQA-irWmQ!!

AAMCO Transmissions
http://www.aamcotransmissions.com/na...g options.html

Air Culnaire (Food Service)
http://www.airculinaire.com/ordering.asp

Alson's Jewelry
http://www.alsonjewelers.com/services.htm

Amherst Technologies
http://www.amherst1.com

Amtech
http://www.amtechdisc.com/payment.htm

ASAP Coach (Limousine Company)
http://www.asapcoach.com/openAccount.htm

AT&T (Phone Services)
www.att.com

A-Vidd Electronics
http://www.a-vidd.com/pdf/aviddcreditapp.pdf

Axion Tech
http://www.axiontech.com/corp.php

Bacario
http://www.bacario.com/Corporate.asp

Ballantye Resort (Hotel)
http://www.ballantyneresort.com/

Bed, Bath & Beyond
http://www.bedbathandbeyond.com/CorpSales.asp?ordernum=-1

Belize Bank (Visa Corporate Credit Account)
(NO PG REQUIRED)
http://www.belizebank.com/pdfs/CorporateCr...Application.pdf

Billing Direct (affiliate program, like CJ.com)
http://www.billingdirect.net/

BladeSmart
http://bladesmart.com/bladesmart.com/statp.../corpsales.html

Bloomingdale's
http://www1.bloomingdales.com/about/hopping/corporate.jsp#

Boston Coach (Limousine Company)
http://www.bostoncoach.com/common/resources/account.jsp

Bridgestreet (Corporate Housing)
www.bridgestreet.com

Carey International (Limousine Company)
www.careyint.com

Cognigen PCs
https://www.cognigen-pc.com/main/ eaccount/c... pplication.aspx

Continental Airlines
http://www.continental.com/programs/uatp/

Corporate Express
http://www.corporateexpress.com/faq.html

Corporate Housing
http://www.corporatehousing.com

Corporate Outfitter
http://corporateoutfitter.cabelas.com

Crestwood Suites (Hotel)
http://www.crestwoodsuites.com/cwdirbill.p...0Bill%20Account

Davel (limousine Company)
www.davel.com

Discount Awards
http://www.discountawards.com/CorpAccounts.asp

Disney
http://disneymeetings.disney.go.com/dwm/ in...oupOverviewPage

DTV City
http://www.dtvcity.com/help/corporate.html

Earthlink Business Services
http://www.earthlink.net/biz/majoraccounts

EBC Computers
http://www.ebccomputers.com/Documents/netterms.PDF

Empire limousine (Limousine Company)
www.empireint.com

Exclusive Tickets
http://www.exclusivetickets.com/corporateInfo.cfm

Fairytale Brownies
http://brownies.com/Corporate%20Credit%20Application.doc

Franklin Sports
http://www.franklinsports.com/fsm/files/cr...application.pdf

FTD.com
http://www.ftd.com/528/corporate/

GAP
http://www.gapincbusinessdirect.com/index.asp

Gempler's
http://www.gemplers.com/a/pages/corpsales.asp

GETTY GAS
http://www.getty.com/gettycardapp.pdf#

Greyhound Bus
www.greyhound.com

Handago
http://www.handango.com/Information.jsp?si...CKey=1 BUSINESS

Harley Davidson
http://www.harley-davidson.com/wcm/
Content/Pages/HDFS/financial services.jsp?locale=en US

Headsets
http://www.headsets.com/headsets/credit/application.html

Hertz
http://www.hertztrucks.com/business/bap.pdf

Hewitt Packard HP
www.hp.com

Hilton Hotels
www.hilton.com

Hunting Bank (Relocation Direct Bill Service)
http://hunting.com/pas/HNB1725.htm

Hyatt Regency lake Tahoe
http://www.cflr.com/courses/ Dir billing.pdf

HydePark Jewelers
http://www.hydeparkjewelers.com/HPSite/dep... application.pdf

IBM Computers
www.ibm.com

Ideal Industries
http://www.idealindustries.com/pdf/EndUserSetUpForm.pdf

Ingram Micro
http://www.ingrammicro.com

Jacopos (Pizzeria)
http://www.jacopos.com/CorporateAccounts.htm

JDR Micro Computers
www.jdr.com/premier

JEB Leasing Company
http://www.jebleasing.com/apply.html

Kohls
http://www.kohlscorporation.com/GiftCard/GiftCards01.htm

Korman Communities (Corporate Housing)
www.korman1.com

L.L. Bean
http://www.llbean.com/corporateSales/?feat=1n

Linens n Things
http://www.1nt.com/corp/index.jsp?page=cor...2corpsalestxt

Luberman's Building
http://www.lumbermens-building.com/ pdf/con...-credit-app.pdf

Luggage Pros
http://www.luggagepros.com

Macys
http://www1.macys.com/store/corporate/index.jsp?bhcp=1

Masters Inn (Hotels)
www.mastersinn.com

Metro Hosting (Web Hosting Provider)
http://www.hostingmetro.com

Mitsubishi Digital Electronics America
http://www.mitsubishi-tv.com/

Monster (They give NET 14 terms)
www.monster.com

Monte Vista
http://www.mvcoop.com/credit/index.asp

My Coffee Supply
http://www.mycoffeesupply.com/corp login.asp

My Tool Store
www.mytoolstore.com

Northwest Builder's Network Inc
http://www.nwbuildnet.com/help/credit.html

Oakwood (Corporate Housing)
www.oakwood.com

Patagonia
http://www.patagonia.com/custserv/corporatesales.html

Peapod food Delivery Service
www.peapod.com

Pioneer Electronics (USA) Inc.
http://www.pioneerelectronics.com/pna/cont...1?fpSiteId=2076

Powell Company
www.powellcompany.com

REI
http://www.rei.com/cgs/?stat=footercorpsales

Rio Pavilion (Hotel)
http://harrahs.com/ourcasinos/rlv/gro...llappform.pdf

Rose City Software
http://www.rosecitysoftware.com/corporate/

Saab
http://www.saabfleet.com/

Sam's Club Credit Account
http://www.onlinecreditcenter2.com/sams/rf...appdirect.html

Samys
http://www.samys.com/industrial.php?PHPSES...8f5165a2082651f

Savoya (Limousine Company)
www.savoya.com

SelectATicket.com
http://www.selectaticket.com/CorporateAccounts.asp

Sencore
http://www.sencore.com/orderinfo/corpopen.htm

Sharper Image
http://www.sharperimage.com/corporatesales/

Sonesta Hotel and Suites
http://www.sonesta.com/coconutgrove/ page.asp?pageID=10904

Staceys
http://www.staceys.com/corporatesales.html

Starbucks
http://www.starbucks.com/business/bizgifts.asp

Super Shuttle (Limousine Company)
http://www.supershuttle.com/webrez/Update.aspx

Surray luggage
http://www.surrayluggage.com/corporatesales.html

Thrifty
http://www.thrifty.com/images/rx/img2076.pdf

Toys R Us
http://www.2toysrus.com/guest/corpSales.cfm.

TradeName.com
http://www.tradename.com/fees/corpacc.html

United States Postal Service
www.usps.com

US Luggage
http://usluggage.com/corpsales.htm

USA Legal Forms
http://www.uslegalforms.com/accountopen.doc

Vac Hut Plus, Inc.
http://www.vachutplus.com/corpacct.htm

Viracon
http://www.viracon.com/corporateCreditApp.html

Waiter.com (food take out company)
http://www.waiter.com/documents/ waiter-corp-account-form.pdf

Walgreens
http://www.walgreens.com/about/community/g...rds/default.jsp

Weems Plath
http://www.weems-plath.com/corporatesales.html

Wilkinson's Flowers
http://www.wilkinsonsflowers.com/help.asp

Williams-Sonoma
www.williams-sonomainc.com/bsa/index.cfm

World lux
http://www.worldlux.com/corporatesales.html

Hotel Resources

Best Western Corporate
6201 No. 24th Parkway
Phoenix, AZ 85014-2023
1-800-780-7234

Comfort Inn Corporate
10750 Columbia Pike
Silver Spring, MD 209001
1-800-228-5150

Country Inn & Suites by Carlson Corporate
11340 Blondo Street Omaha, NE 68164
1-888-201-1746

Courtyard by Marriott Corporate
Marriott Drive
Washington DC 20058
1-800-321-2211

Crown Plaza Corporate
3 Ravinia Drive, Suite 2900
Atlanta, GA 30346
1-800-227-6963

Days Inn Corporate
1918 8th Avenue, NE, P.O. Box 4090
Aberdeen, SD 57402-4090
1-800-329-7466

Doubletree Corporate
9336 Civic Center Drive
Beverly Hills, CA 90210
1-800-222-Tree

Embassy Suites Corporate
9336 Civic Center Drive
Beverly Hills, CA 90210
1-800-362-2779

Fairfield Inn by Marriott Corporate
Marriott Drive
Washington DC 20058
1-800-228-2800

Four Points Corporate
c/o Starwood Hotels & Resorts
1111 Westchester Avenue White Plains, NY 10604
1-888-625-5144

Hampton Inn & Suites Corporate
9336 Civic Center Drive
Beverly Hills, CA 90210
1-800-426-7866

Hilton Corporate
9336 Civic Center Drive
Beverly Hills, CA 90210
1-800-445-8667

Hilton Garden Inn Corporate
9336 Civic Center Drive
Beverly Hills, CA 90210
1-877-782-9444

Holiday Inn Corporate & Holiday Inn Express
3 Ravinia Drive, Suite 2900
Atlanta, GA 30346-2149
1-800-465-4329

Homewood Suites by Hilton Corporate
9336 Civic Center Drive
Beverly Hills, CA 90210
1-800-225-4663

Howard Johnson International Corporate
P.O. Box 27970
Minneapolis, MN 55427-0970
1-800-406-1411

Hyatt Corporate
200 West Madison Street
Chicago, IL 60606
1-800-233-1234

Inter Continental Hotel Group Corporate
3 Ravinia Drive, Suite 2900
Atlanta, GA 30346-2149
1-877-477-4674

Marriott Hotels & Resorts Corporate
Marriott Drive
Washington DC 20058
1-800-228-9290

Quality Inn Corporate
10750 Columbia Pike
Silver Spring, MD 209001
1-800-424-6423

Radisson Hotels & Resorts Corporate
11340 Blondo Street
Omaha, NE 68164
1-888-201-1718

Renaissance Hotels & Resorts Corporate
Marriott Drive
Washington DC 20058
1-800-468-3571

Residence Inn by Marriott Corporate
Marriott Drive
Washington, DC 20058
1-800-331-3131

Sheraton Hotels Corporate c/o Starwood Hotels & Resorts Worldwide, Inc.
1111 Westchester Avenue
White Plains, NY 10604
1-888-625-5144

Staybridge Suites Corporate
3 Ravinia Drive Suite
2900 Atlanta, GA 30346

Phone Contacts

Best Buy – Status: 1-800-811-7276

Borders: 734-477-1039 (Fax Application: 1-877-254-9229; Status Update)

BP/Amoco Status Update: 1-800-365-6204 Chevron/Texaco Business Card Status Update: 1-888-243-8358

Citi AA: 1-888-662-7759

Citibank Status: 1-800-654-7240, 1-800-288-4653, 1-800-750-7453

Conoco Automated Status line: 1-866-289-5622

Experian Business: 1-888-211-0728

Exxon Mobile Business Card: 1-800-903-9966

HD Commercial: 1-800-685-6691

HDMC Sondee: 1-877-969-9030

Home Depot Master Card: 1-877-969-9039

Key Bank: 1-800-254-2737

Liz Claiborne: 1-212-354-4900

Lowe's Status: 1-800-445-6937

Lowe's fraud/UW: 1-800-444-1408

MBNA: 1-800-673-1044

Meijers Master Card: 1-801-517-5560

Office Depot Automated Status line: 1-800-767-1358, 1-800-729-7744

Office Max Automated Status line: 1-800-283-7674

Philips 66: 1-866-289-5630, 1-800-610-1961

Phillips: 1-801-779-7369

Radio Shack: 1-800-442-7221

Sam's UW: 1-800-301-5546, 1-866-246-4282

Sears Status Line: 1-800-599-9710

Shell Fleet Card Status Update: 1-800-223-3296

Shell: 1-800-223-3296, 1-866-438-7435, 1-800-377-5150

Staples Automated Status line: 1-800-767-1275

Staples: 1-800-767-1291, 1-800-282-5316

Sunoco Corporate Card: 1-800-935-3387, 1-800-278-6626

Sunoco: 1-800-310-4773

Target: 1-800-440-5317

Tiffany: 1-800-770-0800

Valero Account Status: 1-800-324-8464

Valero: 1-877-882-5376

Wal-Mart: 1-800-301-5546

Wal-Mart Underwriting: 1-877-294-7548

Wright Express: 1-888-743-3893

Business Credit Quick Start

1. Incorporate or Form LLC
2. Establish a Permanent Business Address
3. Obtain Federal Employer Identification Number (FEIN) (EIN)
4. Open a Business Bank Account
5. Business Email address
6. Obtain a DUNS Number
7. Comply with Local and State Licensing Laws
8. Business Phone
9. Yellow Pages Listing
10. Apply for the Creditors below after steps above have been taken:

   www.reliable.com

   www.nebs.com

   www.rapidforms.com

   www.uline.com

www.staples.com (make sure you have a phone bill, utility bill or commercial lease before you apply)

www.ibsa.com (interstate battery)

Glossary

Acceleration Clause. A loan term that gives the lender the right to demand immediate payment or to require additional collateral.

Accounts payable. Money you owe to creditors for goods and services that you have already received.

Accounts receivable. Money that customers and clients owe you for goods and services you have already provided.

Balance Sheet. A financial statement that shows your assets, liabilities, and owner's equity in the company as of a specific date.

Capital. The amount of money invested in a business.

Compensating Balance. The amount, usually a percentage of the outstanding loan balance that a lender requires to remain on deposit in a bank account.

Debt Ratio. A representation of a company's debt level. Total liabilities divided by total liabilities plus capital.

Equity. The owners interest in the business.

Factoring. A type of financing based on accounts receivable.

Finance Companies. Businesses that provide capital to firms; competitors of banks.

Financial Statement. Records displaying a company's financial condition, such as the profit and loss statement, balance sheet, and cash flow statement.

Gross Profit. Revenues before operating expenses. Net sales less the cost of goods sold for inventory based businesses or net sales for service based businesses.

Letter of Credit. An arrangement where a lender guarantees your payment to a third party.

Line of Credit. A lenders promise to advance funds to a company up to a pre-set limit within a specific time. The line revolves, and more can be borrowed as funds are repaid.

Liquid Assets. Assets that can readily be converted to cash such as a certificate of deposit.

Marketable Securities. Securities that can be readily sold such as stocks and bonds traded on a public exchange.

Net Income. The amount of income remaining after expenses have been paid.

Net Terms. Payments are applied to specific invoices. A monthly statement with invoices attached with balance normally within 30 days after the statement date. Read your invoice carefully because some companies may be net 10, 15 or 20.

Net Sales. Sales minus returns and allowances.

Net Worth. The excess of assets over liabilities.

Profit. What an owner hopes to reap from operating a business.

Profit and Loss Statement. A financial statement showing revenues, cost and expenses of a company over a period of time.

Pro forma financial Statement. A financial statement that includes estimated or hypothetical amounts.

Revolving Account. Payments are applied to the total balance, not specific invoices. One can pay his/her balance in full when due, or, to help manage cash flow, make minimum monthly payments with finance charges.

Security Agreement. A type of financing based on tangible assets, such as equipment or machinery.

Standard Industrial Classification (SIC). A system that the government uses for classifying businesses.

Uniform Commercial Code (UCC). A law that states uses to govern sales and secured transactions and provides standard forms for secured financing transactions.

Bibliography

Internal Revenue Service

1-800-829-4933 for Business www.irs.gov

Dun & Bradstreet

The D&B Corporation

103 JFK Parkway

Short Hills, NJ 0707 www.dnb.com

Office Suite Plus

770-933-6222 www.officesuitesplus.com

Experian
Direct Marketing Services
1-800-588-3657 www.experian.com

HQ Global Workplaces
1-800-956-9543 www.hq.com

National Association of Credit Management
8840 Columbia 100 Parkway
Columbia, MD 21045
Telephone: 410-740-5560
Fax: 410-740-5574 http://www.nacm.org

Made in the USA
Coppell, TX
22 December 2019